D1637487

CARTESIAN MEDITATIONS

Kluwer Translations of Edmund Husserl

Cartesian Meditations. An Introduction to Phenomenology
Translated by Dorion Cairns. xii, 158pp.   PB ISBN 90-247-0068-X

Formal and Transcendental Logic
Translated by Dorion Cairns. xx, 340pp.   PB ISBN 90-247-2052-4

Introduction to the Logical Investigations. A Draft of a 'Preface' to the
'Logical Investigations' (1913)
Edited by Eugen Fink. Translated with Introductions by P.J. Bossert and C.H.
Peters. xxx, 62pp.   PB ISBN 90-247-1711-6

The Idea of Phenomenology
Translated by W.P. Alston and G. Nakhnikian. xxii, 60pp. PB ISBN 20-247-0114-7

The Paris Lectures
Translated with an Introductory Essay by Peter Koestenbaum. Appendix:
General Summary translated with Notes by Steven J. Bartlett. lxxviii, 58pp.
       PB ISBN 90-247-5133-0

Phenomenological Psychology. Lectures, Summer Semester 1925.
Translated by John Scanlon. xvi, 186pp.   PB ISBN 90-247-1978-X

*

**Ideas Pertaining to a Pure Phenomenology and a Phenomenological
Philosophy**
First Book: General Introduction to a Pure Phenomenology
Translated by Fred Kersten, xxiv, 402pp.   PB ISBN 90-247-2852-5
       Cloth ISBN 90-247-2503-8

Second Book: Studies in the Phenomenology of Constitution
Translated by Richard Rojcewicz and André Schuwer. xx, 440pp.
       PB ISBN 90-247-0713-5
       Cloth ISBN 90-247-0011-4

Third Book. Phenomenology and the Foundation of the Sciences.
Translated by Ted E. Klein and William E. Pohl. xviii,130pp.
       Cloth ISBN 90-247-2093-1

Husserl, E.: On the phenomenology of the Consciousness of Internal Time
(1893–1917).
Translated and edited by John Barnett Brough.   PB ISBN 0-7923-1536-7.

EDMUND HUSSERL

Cartesian Meditations
An Introduction to Phenomenology

Translated by
DORION CAIRNS

Kluwer Academic Publishers
Dordrecht / Boston / London

ISBN 90-247-0068-X

Published by Kluwer Academic Publishers,
P.O. Box 17, 3300 AA Dordrecht, The Netherlands.

Kluwer Academic Publishers incorporates the publishing programmes of
D. Reidel, Martinus Nijhoff, Dr W. Junk and MTP Press.

Sold and distributed in the U.S.A. and Canada
by Kluwer Academic Publishers,
101 Philip Drive, Norwell, MA 02061, U.S.A.

In all other countries, sold and distributed
by Kluwer Academic Publishers Group,
P.O. Box 322, 3300 AH Dordrecht, The Netherlands.

Book information:
Originally published in 1950
by Martinus Nijhoff, The Hague, The Netherlands

7th impression 1988, Kluwer Academic Publishers
8th impression 1991, Kluwer Academic Publishers
9th impression 1993, Kluwer Academic Publishers
10th impression 1995, Kluwer Academic Publishers
11th impression 1997, Kluwer Academic Publishers
12th impression 1999, Kluwer Academic Publishers

12-1099-600 ts

Husserl

NOTE

This translation is based primarily on the printed text, edited by Professor S. Strasser and published in the first volume of *Husserliana* (Haag, Martinus Nijhoff, 1950). Most of Husserl's emendations, as given in the Appendix to that volume, have been treated as if they were part of the text. The others have been translated in footnotes.

Secondary consideration has been given to a typescript (cited as "Typescript C") on which Husserl wrote in 1933: "Cartes. Meditationen / Originaltext 1929 / E. Husserl / für Dorion Cairns". Its use of emphasis and quotation marks conforms more closely to Husserl's practice, as exemplified in works published during his lifetime. In this respect the translation usually follows Typescript C. Moreover, some of the variant readings in this typescript are preferable and have been used as the basis for the translation. Where that is the case, the published text is given or translated in a foornote.

The published text and Typescript C have been compared with the French translation by Gabrielle Peiffer and Emmanuel Levinas (Paris, Armand Collin, 1931). The use of emphasis and quotation marks in the French translation corresponds more closely to that in Typescript C than to that in the published text. Often, where the wording of the published text and that of Typescript C differ, the French translation indicates that it was based on a text that corresponded more closely to one or the other — usually to Typescript C. In such cases the French translation has been quoted or cited in a foornote.

CONTENTS

§ 1. *Descartes'* Meditations *as the prototype of philosophical reflection.*

I have particular reason for being glad that I may talk about transcendental phenomenology in this, the most venerable abode of French science.[1] France's greatest thinker, René Descartes, gave transcendental phenomenology new impulses through his *Meditations*; their study acted quite directly on the transformation of an already developing phenomenology into a new kind of transcendental philosophy. Accordingly one might almost call transcendental phenomenology a neo-Cartesianism, even though it is obliged — and precisely by its radical development of Cartesian motifs — to reject nearly all the well-known doctrinal content of the Cartesian philosophy.

That being the situation, I can already be assured of your interest if I start with those motifs in the *Meditationes de prima philosophia* that have, so I believe, an eternal significance and go on to characterize the transformations, and the novel formations, in which the method and problems of transcendental phenomenology originate.

Every beginner in philosophy knows the remarkable train of thoughts contained in the *Meditations*. Let us recall its guiding idea. The aim of the *Meditations* is a complete reforming of philosophy into a science grounded on an absolute foundation. That implies for Descartes a corresponding reformation of all the sciences, because in his opinion they are only non-selfsufficient members of the one all-inclusive science, and this is philosophy. Only within the systematic unity of philosophy can they develop into genuine sciences. As they have developed

---

[1] Translator's note: The *Meditations* are an elaboration of two lectures, entitled *"Einleitung in die transzendentale Phänomenologie"* (Introduction to Transcendental Phenomenology), that Husserl delivered at the Sorbonne on the twenty-third and twenty-fifth of February, 1929. See Strasser's introduction, *Husserliana*, Vol. I, p. XXIII.

‹44› historically, on the other hand, / they lack that scientific genuineness which would consist in their complete and ultimate grounding on the basis of absolute insights, insights behind which one cannot go back any further. Hence the need for a radical rebuilding that satisfies the idea of philosophy as the all-inclusive unity of the sciences, within the unity of such an absolutely [1] rational grounding. With Descartes this demand gives rise to a philosophy turned toward the subject himself. The turn to the subject is made at two significant levels.

First, anyone who seriously intends to become a philosopher must "once in his life" withdraw into himself and attempt, within himself, to overthrow and build anew all the sciences that, up to then, he has been accepting. Philosophy — wisdom (*sagesse*) — is the philosophizer's quite personal affair. It must arise as *his* wisdom, as his self-acquired knowledge tending toward universality, a knowledge for which he can answer from the beginning, and at each step, by virtue of his own absolute insights. If I have decided to live with this as my aim — the decision that alone can start me on the course of a philosophical development — I have thereby chosen to begin in absolute poverty, with an absolute lack of knowledge. Beginning thus, obviously one of the first things I ought to do is reflect on how I might find a method for going on, a method that promises to lead to genuine knowing. Accordingly the Cartesian *Meditations* are not intended to be a merely private concern of the philosopher Descartes, to say nothing of their being merely an impressive literary form in which to present the foundations of his philosophy. Rather they draw the prototype for any beginning philosopher's necessary meditations, the meditations out of which alone a philosophy can grow originally.[2]

---

[1] Supplied in accordance with Typescript C. Cf. the French: "*sur un fondement d'un caractère absolu*".

[2] Author's note: For confirmation of this interpretation see *Lettre de l'auteur* to the translator of the *Principia* (Descartes, *Oeuvres*, Adam and Tannery edition, Vol. IX, 1904, Part 2, pp. 1–20).

Appended later: If someone were to object that, on the contrary, science, philosophy, takes its rise in the cooperative labor of the scientific community of philosophers and, at each level, acquires its perfection only therein, Descartes' answer might well be: I, the solitary individual philosophizer, owe much to others; but what they accept as true, what they offer me as allegedly established by their insight, is for me at first only something they claim. If I am to accept it, I must justify it by a perfect insight on my own part. Therein consists my autonomy — mine and that of every genuine scientist.

When we turn to the content of the *Meditations*, so strange to us men of today, we find a regress to / the philosophizing ‹ 45› ego [1] in a second and deeper sense: the ego as subject of his pure *cogitationes*. The meditator executes this regress by the famous and very remarkable method of doubt. Aiming with radical consistency at absolute knowledge, he refuses to let himself accept anything as existent unless it is secured against every conceivable possibility of becoming doubtful. Everything that is certain, in his natural experiencing and thinking life, he therefore subjects to methodical criticism with respect to the conceivability of a doubt about it; and, by excluding everything that leaves open any possibility of doubt, he seeks to obtain a stock of things that are absolutely evident. When this method is followed, the certainty of sensuous experience, the certainty with which the world is given in natural living, does not withstand criticism; accordingly the being of the world must remain unaccepted at this initial stage. The meditator keeps only himself, qua pure ego of his *cogitationes*, as having an absolutely indubitable existence, as something that cannot be done away with, something that would exist even though this world were non-existent. Thus reduced, the ego carries on a kind of solipsistic philosophizing. He seeks apodictically certain ways by which, within his own pure inwardness, an Objective [2] outwardness can be deduced. The course of the argument is well known: First God's existence and veracity are deduced and then, by means of them, Objective Nature, the duality of finite substances — in short, the Objective field of metaphysics and the positive sciences, and these disciplines themselves. All the various inferences proceed, as they must, according to guiding principles that are immanent, or "innate", in the pure ego.

[1] Translator's note: Sometimes Husserl uses *Ego* and *Ich* to express different senses. Since the homophony of *I* and *eye* makes the English noun *I* intolerable, *Ich* has been translated as *Ego* (spelled with a capital) and *Ego* has been translated as *ego* (spelled with a small letter).

[2] Translator's note: Husserl frequently uses the words *Gegenstand* and *Objekt* to express importantly different senses. Having found no acceptable alternative to translating them both as *object*, I differentiate by spelling this word with a small letter when it represents *Gegenstand* and with a capital when it represents *Objekt*. All this applies, *mutatis mutandis*, in the case of any word derived from *Gegenstand* or *Objekt*. If the English word *object*, or a word derived from it, stands first in a sentence, the German word is given in brackets.

§ 2. *The necessity of a radical new beginning*
of philosophy.

Thus far, Descartes. We ask now: It is really worth while to
hunt for an eternal significance belonging to these thoughts or
to some clarifiable core that may be contained in them? Are
they still such thoughts as might infuse our times with living
forces?

Doubt is raised at least by the fact that the positive sciences,
which were to experience an absolutely rational grounding by
these meditations, have paid so little attention to them. To be
sure, the positive sciences, after three centuries of brilliant development, are now feeling themselves greatly hampered by ob-
scurities in their foundations, in their fundamental concepts and
methods. But, when they attempt to give those foundations a
‹46› new form, they do not think / of turning back to resume Cartesian meditations. On the other hand, great weight must be given
to the consideration that, in philosophy, the *Meditations* were
epoch-making in a quite unique sense, and precisely because of
their going back to the pure *ego cogito*. Descartes, in fact, in-
augurates an entirely new kind of philosophy. Changing its total
style, phiiosophy takes a radical turn: from naïve Objectivism
to transcendental subjectivism — which, with its ever new but
always inadequate attempts, seems to be striving toward some
necessary final form, wherein its true sense and that of the
radical transmutation itself might become disclosed. Should not
this continuing tendency imply an eternal significance and, for
us, a task imposed by history itself, a great task in which we
are all summoned to collaborate?

The splintering of present-day philosophy, with its perplexed
activity, sets us thinking. When we attempt to view western
philosophy as a unitary science, its decline since the middle of
the nineteenth century is unmistakable. The comparative unity
that it had in previous ages, in its aims, its problems and methods,
has been lost. When, with the beginning of modern times, re-
ligious belief was becoming more and more externalized as a
lifeless convention, men of intellect were lifted by a new belief,
their great belief in an autonomous philosophy and science. The
whole of human culture was to be guided and illuminated by

scientific insights and thus reformed, as new and autonomous.

But meanwhile this belief too has begun to languish. Not without reason. Instead of a unitary living philosophy, we have a philosophical literature growing beyond all bounds and almost without coherence [1]. Instead of a serious discussion among conflicting theories that, in their very conflict, demonstrate the intimacy with which they belong together, the commonness of their underlying convictions, and an unswerving belief in a true philosophy, we have a pseudo-reporting and a pseudo-criticizing, a mere semblance of philosophizing seriously with and for one another. This hardly attests a mutual study carried on with a consciousness of responsibility, in the spirit that caracterizes serious / collaboration and an intention to produce Objectively <47> valid results. "Objectively [*objektiv*] valid results" — the phrase, after all, signifies nothing but results that have been refined by mutual criticism and that now withstand every criticism. But how could actual study and actual collaboration be possible, where there are so many philosophers and almost equally many philosophies? To be sure, we still have philosophical congresses. The philosophers meet but, unfortunately, not the philosophies. The philosophies lack the unity of a mental space in which they might exist for and act on one another.[2] It may be that, within each of the many different "schools" or "lines of thought", the situation is somewhat better. Still, with the existence of these in isolation, the total philosophical present is essentially as we have described it.

In this unhappy present, is not our situation similar to the one encountered by Descartes in his youth? If so, then is not this a fitting time to renew his radicalness, the radicalness of the beginning philosopher: to subject to a Cartesian overthrow the immense philosophical literature with its medley of great traditions, of comparatively serious new beginnings, of stylish literary activity (which counts on "making an effect" but not on being studied), and to begin with new *meditationes de prima philosophia*? Cannot the disconsolateness of our philosophical position be traced back ultimately to the fact that the driving

---

[1] Later modified to read: we have an indeed literary, but not seriously scientific, philosophical literature — growing beyond all bounds and without coherence.

[2] The passage beginning "To be sure ..." marked for deletion.

forces emanating from the *Meditations* of Descartes have lost their original vitality — lost it because the spirit that character-izes radicalness of philosophical self-responsibility has been lost? Must not the demand for a philosophy aiming at the ultimate conceivable freedom from prejudice, shaping itself with actual autonomy according to ultimate evidences it has itself produced, and therefore absolutely self-responsible — must not this de-mand, instead of being excessive, be part of the fundamental sense of genuine philosophy? In recent times the longing for a fully alive philosophy has led to many a renaissance. Must not the only fruitful renaissance be the one that reawakens the impulse of the Cartesian *Meditations:* not to adopt their content but, in *not* doing so, to renew with greater intensity the radi-calness of their spirit, the radicalness of self-responsibility, to make that radicalness true for the first time by enhancing it to

‹48› the last degree, / to uncover thereby for the first time the genuine sense of the necessary regress to the ego, and consequently to overcome the hidden but already felt naïveté of earlier phi-losophizing?

In any case, the question indicates one of the ways that has led to transcendental phenomenology.

Along that way we now intend to walk together. In a quasi-Cartesian fashion we intend, as radically beginning philosophers, to carry out meditations with the utmost critical precaution and a readiness for any — even the most far-reaching — transfor-mation of the old-Cartesian meditations. Seductive aberrations, into which Descartes and later thinkers strayed, will have to be clarified and avoided as we pursue our course.

FIRST MEDITATION

THE WAY TO THE TRANSCENDENTAL EGO

§ 3. *The Cartesian overthrow and the guiding final idea of an absolute* [1] *grounding of science*

And so we make a new beginning, each for himself and in himself, with the decision of philosophers who begin radically: that at first we shall put out of action all the convictions we have been accepting up to now, including all our sciences. Let the idea guiding our meditations be at first the Cartesian idea of a science that shall be established as radically genuine, ultimately an all-embracing science.

But, now that we no longer have at our disposal any already-given science as an example of radically genuine science (after all, we are not accepting any given science), what about the indubitability of that idea itself, the idea namely of a science that shall be grounded absolutely? Is it a legitimate final idea, the possible aim of some possible practice? Obviously that too is something we must not presuppose, to say nothing of taking any norms as already established for testing such possibilities — or perchance a whole system of norms in which the style proper to genuine science is allegedly prescribed. That would mean presupposing a whole logic as a theory of science; whereas logic must be included among the sciences overthrown in overthrowing all science. Descartes himself presupposed an ideal of science, the ideal approximated by geometry and mathematical natural science. As a fateful / prejudice this ideal determines philoso- ‹49› phies for centuries and hiddenly determines the *Meditations* themselves. Obviously it was, for Descartes, a truism from the start that the all-embracing science must have the form of a deductive system, in which the whole structure rests, *ordine geometrico*, on an axiomatic foundation that grounds the deduction absolutely. For him a role similar to that of geometrical axioms in geometry is played in the all-embracing science

[1] Supplied in accordance with Typescript C and the French translation.

by the axiom of the ego's absolute certainty of himself, along with the axiomatic principles innate in the ego — only this axiomatic foundation lies even deeper than that of geometry and is called on to participate in the ultimate grounding even of geometrical knowledge.[1]

None of that shall determine our thinking. As beginning philosophers we do not as yet accept any normative ideal of science, and only so far as we produce one newly for ourselves can we ever have such an ideal.

But this does not imply that we renounce the general aim of grounding science absolutely. That aim shall indeed continually motivate the course of our meditations, as it motivated the course of the Cartesian meditations; and gradually, in our meditations, it shall become determined concretely. Only we must be careful about how we make an absolute grounding of science our aim. At first we must not presuppose even its possibility. How then are we to find the legitimate manner in which to make it our aim? How are we to make our aim perfectly assured, and thus assured as a practical possibility? How are we then to differentiate the possibility, into which at first we have a general insight, and thereby mark out the determinate methodical course of a genuine philosophy, a radical philosophy that begins with what is intrinsically first?

Naturally we get the general idea of science from the sciences that are factually given. If they have become for us, in our radical critical attitude, merely alleged sciences, then, according to what has already been said, their general final idea has become, in a like sense, a mere supposition. Thus we do not yet know whether that idea is at all capable of becoming actualized.[2] Nevertheless we do have it in this form, and in a state of indeterminate fluid generality; accordingly we have also the idea of philosophy: as an idea about which we do not know whether or how it can be actualized.[3] We take the general idea of science, therefore, as a precursory presumption, which we allow ourselves

---

[1] The passage beginning "Obviously it was ..." marked for deletion.
[2] This sentence marked for deletion.
[3] Reading, with Typescript C, *"als unbekannt o b und w i e zu verwirklichende"* instead of *"als einer unbekannt ob und wie zu verwirklichenden"*. Thus the published text (unlike either Typescript C or the French translation) relates the phrase to *philosophy* rather than to *idea*.

tentatively, by which we tentatively allow ourselves to be guided in our meditations. We consider how it might be thought out as a possibility and then consider whether and how it might be given determinate actualization. To be sure, we get into what are, at first, rather strange circumstantialities — but how can / they be avoided, if our radicalness is not to remain an empty ⟨50⟩ gesture but is to become an actual deed? Let us go on then with patience.

§ 4. *Uncovering the final sense of science*
by becoming immersed in science qua noematic phenomenon.

Obviously one of the first things we must do now is make distinct the guiding idea that, at the beginning, floats before us as a vague generality. The genuine concept of science, naturally, is not to be fashioned by a process of abstraction based on comparing the de facto sciences, i.e. the Objectively documented theoretical structures (propositions, theories) that are in fact generally accepted as sciences. The sense of our whole meditation implies that sciences, as these facts of Objective culture, and sciences "in the true and genuine sense" need not be identical and that the former, over and above being cultural facts, involve a claim, which ought to be established as one they already satisfy. Science as an idea — as the idea, genuine science — "lies", still undisclosed, precisely in this claim.

How can this idea be uncovered and apprehended? Even though we must not take any position with respect to the *validity* of the de facto sciences (the ones "claiming" validity) — i.e. with respect to the genuineness of their theories and, correlatively, the competence of their methods of theorizing — there is nothing to keep us from "immersing ourselves" in the scientific striving and doing that pertain to them, in order to see clearly and distinctly what is really being aimed at. If we do so,[1] if we immerse ourselves progressively in the characteristic intention of scientific endeavor, the constituent parts of the general final idea, genuine science, become explicated for us, though at first the differentiation is itself general.

---

[1] Reading, with Typescript C, "*Tun wir so*", instead of "*Treten wir so*". Cf. the French: "*Si, agissant de la sorte*".

Here belongs, first of all, an initial clarification of *"judicative"* *doing* and the *"judgment"* itself, along with the discrimination of *immediate and mediate judgments:* mediate judgments have such a sense-relatedness to other judgments that judicatively believing them "presupposes" believing these others — in the manner characteristic of a believing on account of something believed already. Also clarification of the striving for *grounded judgments*, clarification of the grounding doing, in which the *"correctness"*, the *"truth"*, of the judgment should be shown —
⟨51⟩ or, in case of a failure, the / incorrectness, the falsity, of the judgment. Where mediate judgments are concerned, this showing is itself mediate; it rests on the showing that pertains to the immediate judgments involved in the judgment-sense and, as concrete, includes their grounding too. To a grounding already executed, or to the truth shown therein, one can "return" at will. By virtue of this freedom to reactualize such a truth, with awareness of it as one and the same, it is an abiding acquisition or possession and, as such, is called a *cognition*.

If we go further in this manner (here, naturally, we are only indicating the procedure), then, in explicating more precisely the sense of a grounding or that of a cognition, we come forthwith to the idea of *evidence*. In a genuine grounding, judgments show themselves as "correct", as "agreeing"; that is to say, the grounding is an *agreement* of the judgment with the judged state of affairs [*Urteilsverhalt*] (the affair or affair-complex [*Sach-verhalt*]) *"itself"*. More precisely stated: Judging is meaning — and, as a rule, merely supposing — that such and such exists and has such and such determinations; the judgment (what is judged) is then a merely supposed affair or complex of affairs: an affair, or state-of-affairs, as what is meant. But, contrasted with that, there is sometimes a pre-eminent judicative meaning [*Meinen*], a judicative having of such and such itself. This having is called *evidence*. In it the affair, the complex (or state) of affairs, instead of being merely meant "from afar", is present as the affair *"itself"*, the *affair-complex or state-of-affairs "itself"*; the judger accordingly possesses it itself. A merely supposing judging *be-comes adjusted* to the affairs, the affair-complexes, themselves by conscious conversion into the corresponding evidence. This conversion is inherently characterized as the fulfilling of what was merely meant, a synthesis in which what was meant coincides and agrees with what is itself given; it is an evident possessing of the correctness of what previously was meant at a distance from affairs.

When we proceed thus, fundamental components of the final idea governing all scientific doing come immediately to the fore. For example, the scientist intends, not merely to judge, but to ground his judgments. Stated more precisely: He intends to let no judgment be accepted by himself or others as "scientific knowledge", unless he has grounded it perfectly and can therefore justify it completely at any time by a freely actualizable return to his repeatable act of grounding. De facto that may never go beyond being a mere claim; at all events, the claim involves an ideal goal. /

Yet there is one more thing that should be brought out, to   ‹52›
supplement what we have said. We must distinguish the judgment in the broadest sense (something meant as being) and evidence in the broadest sense from pre-predicative judgment and from pre-predicative evidence respectively. Predicative in cludes pre-predicative evidence. That which is meant or, perchance, evidently viewed receives predicative expression; and science always intends to judge expressly and keep the judgment or the truth fixed, as an express judgment or as an express truth. But the expression as such has its own comparatively good or bad way of fitting what is meant or itself given; and therefore it has its own evidence or non-evidence, which also goes into the predicating. Consequently evidence of the expression is also a determining part of the idea of scientific truth, as predicative complexes that are, or can be, grounded absolutely.

§ 5. *Evidence and the idea of genuine science.*

As we go on meditating in this manner and along this line, we beginning philosophers recognize that the Cartesian idea of a science (ultimately an all-embracing science) grounded on an absolute foundation, and absolutely justified, is none other than the idea that constantly furnishes guidance in all sciences and in their striving toward universality — whatever may be the situation with respect to a de facto actualization of that idea.

Evidence is, in an *extremely broad sense,* an *"experiencing"* of something that is, and is thus; it is precisely a mental seeing of something itself. Conflict with what evidence shows, with what "experience" shows, yields the negative of evidence (or negative evidence) — put in the form of a judgment: positive evidence of the affair's non-being. In other words, negative evidence has as its content evident falsity. Evidence, which in fact includes all experiencing in the usual and narrower sense, can be more or less perfect. *Perfect evidence* and its correlate, *pure and genuine truth,* are given as ideas lodged in the striving for knowledge, for fulfilment of one's meaning intention. By immersing ourselves in such a striving, we can extract those ideas from it. Truth and falsity, criticism and critical comparison with evident data, are an everyday theme, playing their incessant part even in pre-scientific life. For this everyday life, with its changing and relative purposes, relative evidences [1] and truths suffice. But science

‹53› | looks for truths that are valid, and remain so, *once for all and for everyone;* accordingly it seeks verifications of a new kind, verifications carried through to the end. Though de facto, as science itself must ultimately see, it does not attain actualization of a system of absolute truths, but rather is obliged to modify its "truths" again and again, it nevertheless follows the idea of absolute or scientifically genuine truth; and accordingly it reconciles itself to an infinite horizon of approximations, tending toward that idea. By them, science believes, it can surpass *in infinitum* not only everyday knowing but also itself; likewise however by its aim at systematic universality of knowledge, whether that aim concern a particular closed scientific province or a presupposed all-embracing unity of whatever exists — as it does if a "philosophy" is possible and in question. According to intention, therefore, the idea of science and philosophy involves an *order of cognition, proceeding from intrinsically earlier to intrinsically later cognitions;* ultimately, then, *a beginning and a line of advance* that are not to be chosen arbitrarily but have their basis "in the nature of things themselves".

Thus, by immersing ourselves meditatively in the general in-

---

[1] Author's marginal note: They are relative, inasmuch as the sense of the everyday judgment, made at a particular time, relates that judgment to the judger's circumstances on that occasion.

tentions of scientific endeavor, we discover fundamental parts of the final idea, genuine science, which, though vague at first, governs that striving. Meanwhile we have made no advance judgment in favor of the possibility of those components or in favor of a supposedly unquestionable scientific ideal.

We must not say at this point: "Why bother with such investigations and ascertainments? They obviously belong to the general theory of science, to logic, which must of course be applied both now and later." On the contrary, we must guard ourselves against just this matter-of-course opinion. Let us emphasize what we said against Descartes: Like every other already-given science, logic is deprived of acceptance by the universal overthrow. Everything that makes a philosophical beginning possible we must first acquire by ourselves.[1] Whether, later on, a genuine science similar to traditional logic will accrue to us is an eventuality about which we can at present know nothing.

By this / preliminary work, here roughly indicated rather than ‹54› done explicitly, we have gained a measure of clarity sufficient to let us fix, for our whole further procedure, a *first methodological principle*. It is plain that I, as someone beginning philosophically, since I am striving toward the presumptive end, genuine science, must neither make nor go on accepting any judgment as scientific *that I have not derived from evidence*, from "experiences" in which the affairs and affair-complexes in question are present to me as *"they themselves"*. Indeed, even then I must at all times reflect on the pertinent evidence; I must examine its "range" and make evident to myself *how far* that evidence, how far its "perfection", *the actual giving of the affairs themselves*, extends. Where this is still wanting, I must not claim any final validity, but must account my judgment as, at best, a possible intermediate stage on the way to final validity.

Because the sciences aim at predications that express completely and with evident fitness what is beheld pre-predicatively, it is obvious that I must be careful also about this aspect of scientific evidence. Owing to the instability and ambiguity

---

[1] Reading with Typescript C and the French translation. The published text may be rendered: "All that has been developed as beginnings of philosophy we must first acquire by ourselves."

of common language and its much too great complacency about completeness of expression, we require, even where we use its means of expression, a new legitimation of significations by orienting them according to accrued insights, and a fixing of words as expressing the significations thus legitimated. That too we account as part of our normative principle of evidence, which we shall apply consistently from now on.

But how would this principle, or all our meditation up to now, help us, if it gave us no hold for making an actual beginning, that is, for starting to actualize the idea of genuine science? Since the form belonging to a systematic order of cognitions — genuine cognitions — is part of this idea, there emerges, as the *question of the beginning*, the inquiry for those cognitions that are first in themselves and can support the whole storied edifice of universal knowledge. Consequently, if our presumptive aim is to be capable of becoming a practically possible one, we meditators, while completely destitute of all scientific knowledge, must have ‹ 55 › access to evidences that already / bear the stamp of fitness for such a function, in that they are recognizable as preceding all other imaginable evidences.[1] Moreover, in respect of this evidence of preceding, they must have a certain perfection, they must carry with them an absolute certainty, if advancing from them and constructing on their basis a science governed by the idea of a definitive system of knowledge — considering the infinity presumed to be part of this idea — is to be capable of having any sense.

§ 6. *Differentiations of evidence. The philosophical demand for an evidence that is apodictic and first in itself.*

But here, at this decisive point in the process of beginning, we must penetrate deeper with our meditations. The phrase *absolute certainty* and the equivalent phrase *absolute indubitability* need clarifying. They call our attention to the fact that, on more precise explication, the ideally demanded *perfection of evidence becomes differentiated*. At the present introductory stage of philosophical meditation we have the boundless infinity of prescientific experiences, evidences: more or less perfect. With

---

[1] Author's marginal note: As founding evidences! And absolutely certain.

reference to them *imperfection*, as a rule, signifies *incompleteness*, a one-sidedness and at the same time a relative obscurity and indistinctness that qualify the givenness of the affairs themselves or the affair-complexes themselves: i.e., an infectedness of the ,,experience" with *unfulfilled components*, with *expectant* and *attendant meanings*.[1] Perfecting then takes place as a synthetic course of further harmonious experiences in which these attendant meanings become fulfilled in actual experience. The corresponding idea of perfection would be that of *"adequate evidence"* — and the question whether adequate evidence does not necessarily lie at infinity may be left open.[2]

Though this idea continuously guides the scientist's intent, *a different perfection* of evidence has for him (as we see by the aforesaid process of "immersing ourselves" in his intent) a higher dignity. This perfection is *"apodicticity"*; and it can occur even in evidences that are inadequate. It is *absolute indubitability* in a quite definite and peculiar sense, the absolute indubiability that the scientist demands of all *"principles"*; and its superior value is evinced in his endeavor, / where groundings ‹56› already evident in and by themselves are concerned, to ground them further and at a higher level by going back to principles, and thereby to obtain for them the highest dignity, that of apodicticity. The fundamental nature of apodicticity can be characterized in the following manner:

Any evidence is a grasping of something itself that is, or is thus, a grasping in the mode "it itself", with full certainty of its being, a certainty that accordingly excludes every doubt. But it does not follow that full certainty excludes the conceivability that what is evident could subsequently become doubtful, or the conceivability that being could prove to be illusion — indeed, sensuous experience furnishes us with cases where that happens. Moreover, this open possibility of becoming doubtful, or of non-being, *in spite of evidence*, can always be recognized in advance by critical reflection on what the evidence in question does. An *apodictic* evidence, however, is not merely certainty of the affairs or affair-complexes (states-of-affairs) evident in it; rather it discloses itself, to a critical reflection, as having the signal pe-

---

[1] Author's marginal note on this sentence: But that must be shown.
[2] This sentence marked as unsatisfactory.

culiarity of being *at the same time the absolute unimaginableness* (inconceivability) of their *non-being*, and thus excluding in advance every doubt as "objectless", empty. Furthermore the evidence of that critical reflection likewise has the dignity of being apodictic, as does therefore the evidence of the unimaginableness of what is presented with <apodictically> evident certainty. And the same is true of every critical reflection at a higher level.[1]

We remember now the Cartesian principle for building genuine science: the principle of absolute indubitability, by which every imaginable doubt (even though it were in fact groundless) was to be excluded. If, by our meditations, we have acquired that principle in a clarified form, there arises the question whether and how it might help us make an actual beginning. In accordance with what has already been said, we now formulate, as an initial definite question of beginning philosophy, the question whether it is possible for us to bring out evidences that, on the one hand, carry with them – as we now must say: apodictically — the insight that, as "first in themselves", they precede all other imaginable evidences and, on the other hand, can be seen to be themselves apodictic. If they should turn out to be inadequate, they would have to possess at least a recognizable apodictic content, they would have to give us some being that is firmly secured "once for all", or absolutely, by <57> virtue of their apodicticity. *How,* / and even *whether,* it would be possible to go on from there and build an apodictically secured philosophy must, of course, remain for later consideration.[2]

[1] Strasser reports that the passage rendered by the sentences beginning with "An *apodictic* evidence ..." includes emendations made by Fink. The earlier wording given by Strasser may be rendered as follows: "An apodictic evidence, however, has the signal peculiarity that the certainty of the being of what is beheld in it discloses itself, to a critical reflection, as an absolute unimaginableness (inconceivability) of the seen object's non-being and therefore of that object's being dubitable. [Blank space for a word] the evidence of that critical reflection likewise has this dignity of being apodictic. And the same is true at every level of critical reflection and also with respect to always possible apodictic reflections." (Translator's note: The thought underlying the phrase, "with respect to always possible apodictic reflections", may be that one can see apodictically that *apodictic* reflective insight into the apodicticity of any apodictic reflective evidence is always possible.)

[2] Author's marginal note: From here Fink. (Translator's note: Strasser comments: "Yet § 6 already shows numerous improvements by Eugen Fink's hand." The improvements to which Strasser refers were made before the French translation (1931). Husserl's marginal note probably refers to suggestions for revision submitted by Fink in 1932. See Strasser's introduction to *Husserliana*, Vol. 1, p. XXVIII.

§ 7. *The evidence for the factual existence of the world not apodictic; its inclusion in the Cartesian overthrow.*

The question of evidences that are first in themselves can apparently be answered without any trouble. Does not the *existence of the world* present itself forthwith as such an evidence? The life of everyday action relates to the world. All the sciences relate to it: the sciences of matters of fact relate to it immediately; the apriori sciences, mediately, as instruments of scientific method. More than anything else the being of the world is obvious. It is so very obvious that no one would think of asserting it expressly in a proposition. After all, we have our continuous experience in which this world incessantly stands before our eyes, as existing without question. But, however much this evidence is prior in itself to all the ‹other› evidences of life (as turned toward the world) and to all the evidences of all the world sciences (since it is the basis that continually supports them), we soon become doubtful about the extent to which, in this capacity, it can lay claim to being apodictic. And, if we follow up this doubt, it becomes manifest that our experiential evidence of the world lacks also the superiority of being the absolutely primary evidence. Concerning the first point, we note that the universal sensuous experience in whose evidence the world is continuously given to us beforehand is obviously not to be taken forthwith as an apodictic evidence, which, as such, would absolutely exclude both the possibility of eventual doubt whether the world is actual and the possibility of its non-being. Not only can a particular experienced thing suffer devaluation as an illusion of the senses; the whole unitarily surveyable nexus, experienced throughout a period of time, can prove to be an illusion, a coherent dream. We need not take the indicating of these possible and sometimes actual reversals of evidence as a sufficient criticism of the evidence in question and see in it a full proof that, in spite of the continual experiencedness of the world, a non-being of the world is conceivable. We shall retain only this much: that the evidence of world-experience would, at all events, need to be criticized with regard to its validity and range, before it could be used for the purposes of a radical grounding of science, and that therefore

‹58› we / must not take that evidence to be, without question, immediately apodictic. It follows that denying acceptance to all the sciences given us beforehand, treating them as, for us, inadmissible prejudices [1], is not enough. Their universal basis, the experienced world, must also be deprived of its naïve acceptance. The being of the world, by reason of the evidence of natural experience, must no longer be for us an obvious matter of fact; it too must be for us, henceforth, only an acceptance-phenomenon.

If we maintain this attitude, is any being whatever left us as a basis for judgments, let alone for evidences on which we could establish an all-embracing philosophy and, furthermore, do so apodictically? Is not "the world" the name for the universe of whatever exists? If so, how can we avoid starting *in extenso*, and as our first task, that criticism of world-experience which, a moment ago, we merely indicated? Then, if criticism were to yield the result considered likely in advance, would not our whole philosophical aim [2] be frustrated? But what if the world were, in the end, not at all the absolutely first basis for judgments and a being that is intrinsically prior to the world were the already presupposed basis for the existence of the world?

§ 8. *The* ego cogito *as transcendental subjectivity.*

At this point, following Descartes, we make the great reversal that, if made in the right manner, leads to transcendental subjectivity: the turn to the *ego cogito* as the ultimate and apodictically certain basis for judgments, the basis on which any radical philosophy must be grounded.[3]

Let us consider. As radically meditating philosophers, we now have neither a science that we accept nor a world that exists for us. Instead of simply existing for us — that is, being accepted naturally by us in our experiential believing in its existence — the world is for us only something that claims being. Moreover,

---

[1] Supplied in accordance with Typescript C and the French translation.

[2] Reading, with Typescript C, "*Absehen*" instead of "*Ergebnis*" (result). Cf. the French translation: "*entreprise*".

[3] Author's marginal note: It is necessary to say that the reduction has apodictic significance, since it shows apodictically that the being of the transcendental Ego is antecedent to the being of the world.

that affects the intramundane existence of all other Egos,[1] so that rightly we should no longer speak communicatively, in the plural. Other men than I, and brute animals, are data of experience for me only by virtue of my sensuous experience of their bodily organisms; and, since the validity of this experience too is called in question, I must not use it. Along with other Egos, / naturally, I lose all the formations pertaining to sociality and culture. In short, not just corporeal Nature but the whole concrete surrounding life-world is for me, from now on, only a phenomenon of being, instead of something that is. <59>

But, no matter what the status of this phenomenon's claim to actuality and no matter whether, at some future time, I decide critically that the world exists or that it is an illusion, still this phenomenon itself, as mine, is not nothing but is precisely what makes such critical decisions at all possible and accordingly makes possible whatever has for me sense and validity as "true" being — definitively decided or definitively decideable being. And besides: If I abstained — as I was free to do and as I did — and still abstain from every believing involved in or founded on sensuous experiencing,[2] so that the being of the experienced world remains unaccepted by me, still this abstaining is what it is; and it exists, together with the whole stream of my experiencing life. Moreover, this life is continually there *for me*. Continually, in respect of a field of the present, it is given to consciousness perceptually, with the most originary originality, as it itself; memorially, now these and now those pasts thereof are "again" given to consciousness, and that implies: as the "pasts themselves". Reflecting, I can at any time look at this original living and note particulars; I can grasp what is present as present, what is past as past, each as itself. I do so now, as the Ego who philosophizes and exercises the aforesaid abstention.

Meanwhile the world experienced in this reflectively grasped life goes on being for me (in a certain manner) "experienced" as before, and with just the content it has at any particular time. It goes on appearing, as it appeared before; the only difference is that I, as reflecting philosophically, no longer keep in effect

---

[1] Author's marginal note: Likewise the intramundane existence of my own Ego as human!

[2] Reading with Typescript C. According to the published text and the French translation: "every experiential believing".

(no longer accept) the natural believing in existence involved in experiencing the world [1] — though that believing too is still there and grasped by my noticing regard.[2] The same is true of all the processes of meaning that, in addition to the world-experiencing [3] ones, belong to my lifestream: the non-intuitive processes of meaning objects, the judgings, valuings, and decidings, the processess of setting ends and willing means, and all the rest, in particular the position-takings necessarily involved in them all when I am in the natural and non-reflective attitude — since precisely these position-takings always presuppose the world, i.e., involve believing in its existence. Here too / the philosophically reflective Ego's absention from position-takings, his depriving them of acceptance, does not signify their disappearance from his field of experience. The concrete subjective processes, let us repeat, are indeed the things to which his attentive regard is directed: but the attentive Ego, qua philosophizing [4] Ego, practices abstention with respect to what he intuits. Likewise everything *meant* in such accepting or positing processes of consciousness (the meant judgment, theory, value, end, or whatever it is) is still retained completely — but with the acceptance-modification, "mere phenomenon".

This universal depriving of acceptance, this "inhibiting" or "putting out of play" of all positions taken toward the already-given Objective world and, in the first place, all existential positions (those concerning being, illusion, possible being, being likely, probable, etc.), — or, as it is also called, this "phenomenological epoché" and "parenthesizing" of the Objective world — therefore does not leave us confronting nothing. On the contrary we gain possession of something by it; and what we (or, to speak more precisely, what I, the one who is meditating) acquire by it is my pure living, with all the pure subjective processes making this up, and everything meant in them, *purely as* meant in them: the universe of "phenomena" in the (particular and

‹60›

---

[1] The phrase "the world" supplied in accordance with Typescript C.

[2] Author's marginal note: Background, habitual accepting, etc., do not seem to be taken into consideration.

[3] Reading with Typescript C. According to the published text and the French translation, simply "experiencing".

[4] Reading, with Typescript C, *"philosophierendes"* instead of *"philosophisches"* (philosophical).

also the wider) [1] phenomenological sense. The epoché can also be said to be the radical and universal method by which I apprehend myself purely: as Ego, and with my own pure conscious life, in and by which the entire Objective world exists for me and is precisely as it is for me. Anything belonging to the world, any spatiotemporal being, exists for me — that is to say, is accepted by me — in that I experience it, perceive it, remember it, think of it somehow, judge about it, value it, desire it, or the like. Descartes, as we know, indicated all that by the name *cogito*. The world is for me absolutely nothing else but the world existing for and accepted by me in such a conscious *cogito*. It gets its whole sense, universal and specific, and its acceptance as existing, exclusively from such *cogitationes*.[2] In these my whole world-life goes on, including my scientifically inquiring and grounding life. By my living, by my experiencing, thinking, valuing, and acting, I can enter no world other than the one that gets its sense and acceptance or status [*Sinn und Geltung*] in and from me, myself. If I put myself above all this life and / refrain from doing any believing that takes "the" world ‹61› straightforwardly as existing — if I direct my regard exclusively to this life itself, as consciousness *of* "the" world — I thereby acquire myself as the pure [3] ego, with the pure stream of my *cogitationes*.

Thus the being of the pure ego and his *cogitationes*, as a being that is prior in itself, is antecedent to the natural being of the world — the world of which I always speak, the one of which I *can* speak. Natural being is a realm whose existential status [*Seinsgeltung*] is secondary; it continually presupposes the realm of transcendental being. The fundamental phenomenological method of transcendental epoché, because it leads back to this realm, is called transcendental-phenomenological reduction.[4]

---

[1] Supplied in accordance with Typescript C and the French translation.
[2] Author's marginal note: But if something becomes for me an illusion.
[3] Author's marginal note: Pure in the transcendental sense. This purity I shall call transcendental purity.
[4] Author's marginal note: There seems to be lacking the apodicticity of the precedence belonging to transcendental subjectivity.

§ 9. *The range covered by apodictic evidence of the "I am".*

The next question is whether this reduction makes possible an *apodictic* evidence of the being of transcendental subjectivity. Only if my experiencing of my transcendental self is apodictic can it serve as ground and basis for apodictic judgments; only then is there accordingly the prospect of a philosophy, a systematic structure made up of apodictic cognitions, starting with the intrinsically first field of experience and judgment. That *ego sum* or *sum cogitans* must be pronounced apodictic, and that accordingly we get a first apodictically existing basis to stand on, was already seen by Descartes. As we all know, he emphasizes the indubitability of that proposition and stresses the fact that "I doubt" would itself presuppose "I am". For Descartes too it is a matter of that Ego who grasps himself after he has deprived the experienced world of acceptance, because it might be doubtful. After our differentiations, it is clear that the sense of the indubitability with which the ego becomes given by transcendental reduction actually conforms to the concept of apodicticity we explicated earlier. To be sure, the problem of apodicticity — and consequently the problem of the primary basis on which to ground a philosophy — is not thereby removed. In fact, doubt arises immediately. For example: Does not transcendental subjectivity at any given moment include its past as an inseparable part, which is accessible only by way of <62> memory? But can / apodictic evidence be claimed for memory? Assuredly it would be wrong to deny the apodicticity of "I am", on the ground that the evidence of memory is not apodictic; such a denial is possible only if one confines oneself to arguing about that apodicticity — that is to say, if one shuts one's eyes to it. Nevertheless, in view of such questions, the problem of the range covered by our apodictic evidence becomes urgent.

We remember in this connexion an earlier remark: that *adequacy and apodicticity* of evidence *need not go hand in hand*. Perhaps this remark was made precisely with the case of transcendental self-experience in mind. In such experience the ego is accessible to himself originaliter. But at any particular time this experience offers only a core that is experienced "with strict adequacy", namely the ego's living present (which the grammatical sense of the sentence, *ego cogito*, expresses); while, beyond that, only an indeterminately general presumptive horizon extends, comprising what is strictly non-experienced but necessarily also-meant. To it belongs not only the ego's past, most of which is completely obscure, but also his transcendental abilities and his habitual peculiarities at the time. External perception too (though not apodictic) is an experiencing of something itself, the physical thing itself: "it itself is there". But, in being there itself, the physical thing has for the experiencer an open, infinite, indeterminately general horizon, comprising what is itself not strictly perceived — a horizon (this is implicit as a presumption) that can be opened up by possible experiences. Something similar is true about the apodictic certainty characterizing transcendental experience of my transcendental I-am, with the indeterminate generality of the latter as having an open horizon. Accordingly the actual being of the intrinsically first field of knowledge is indeed assured absolutely, though not as yet what determines its being more particularly and is still not itself given, but only presumed, during the living evidence of the I-am. This presumption implicit in the apodictic evidence is subject therefore to criticism, regarding the possibilities of its fulfilment and their range (which may be apodictically determinable). How far can the transcendental ego be deceived about himself? And how far do those components extend that are absolutely indubitable, in spite of such possible deception?

When making certain of the transcendental ego, we are standing at / an altogether dangerous point, even if at first we <63> leave out of consideration the difficult question of apodicticity.

§ 10. *Digression: Descartes' failure to make
the transcendental turn.*

It seems so easy, following Descartes, to lay hold of the pure Ego and his *cogitationes*. And yet it is as though we were on the brink of a precipice, where advancing calmly and surely is a matter of philosophical life and death. Descartes had the serious will to free himself radically from prejudice. But we know from recent inquiries, in particular the fine and profound researches

of Mr. Gilson and Mr. Koyré,[1] how much scholasticism lies
hidden, as unclarified prejudice, in Descartes' *Meditations*. Not
only that. In the first place we must stay clear of the previously
mentioned prejudice, arising from admiration of mathematical
natural science and, as an old heritage, exercising a determining
influence even on us: the prejudice that, under the name *ego
cogito*, one is dealing with an apodictic "axiom", which, in con-
junction with other axioms and, perhaps, inductively grounded
hypotheses, is to serve as the foundation for a deductively "ex-
planatory" world-science, a "nomological" science, a science
ordine geometrico, similar indeed to mathematical natural science.
In this connexion, furthermore, it must by no means be accepted
as a matter of course that, with our apodictic pure ego, we have
rescued a little *tag-end of the world*, as the sole unquestionable
part of it for the philosophizing Ego, and that now the problem
is to infer the rest of the world by rightly conducted arguments,
according to principles innate in the ego.

Unfortunately these prejudices were at work when Descartes
introduced the apparently insignificant but actually fateful
change whereby the ego becomes a *substantia cogitans*, a separate
human *"mens sive animus"*,[2] and the point of departure for
inferences according to the principle of causality — in short, the
change by virtue of which Descartes became the father of
transcendental realism, an absurd position, though its absurdity
cannot be made apparent at this point. We remain aloof from
all that, if we remain true to the radicalness of our meditative
self-examination and therefore to the principle of pure "intuition" or evidence — that is to say, if we accept nothing here but
‹64› what we / find actually given (and, at first, quite immediately [3])
in the field of the *ego cogito*, which has been opened up to us by
epoché, and if accordingly we assert nothing we ourselves do
not "see". Descartes erred in this respect. Consequently he stands
on the threshold of the greatest of all discoveries — in a certain
manner, has already made it — yet he does not grasp its proper

---

[1] Translator's note: Etienne Gilson, *Études sur le rôle de la pensée médiévale dans
la formation du système cartésien* (Paris, 1930), and Alexandre Koyré, *Essai sur
l'idée de dieu et sur les preuves de son existence chez Descartes* (Paris, 1922).

[2] Author's marginal note: And, in his opinion, even a pure *intellectus*, allegedly
thinkable as an *intellectus* without any imagination.

[3] Author's marginal note: And then mediately; but mediate givenness is not
always deduction.

sense, the sense namely of transcendental subjectivity, and so he does not pass through the gateway that leads into genuine transcendental philosophy.

§ 11. *The psychological and the transcendental Ego.*
The transcendency of the world.

If I keep purely what comes into view — for me, the one who is meditating — by virtue of my free epoché with respect to the being of the experienced world, the momentous fact is that I, with my life, remain untouched [1] in my existential status, regardless of whether or not the world exists and regardless of what my eventual decision concerning its being or non-being might be. This Ego, with his Ego-life, who necessarily remains [2] for me, by virtue of such epoché, is not a piece of the world; and if he says, "I exist, *ego cogito*," that no longer signifies, "I, this man, exist." [3] No longer am I the man who, in natural self-experience, finds himself *as* a man and who, with the abstractive restriction to the pure contents of "internal" or purely psychological self-experience, finds his own pure *"mens sive animus sive intellectus"*; nor am I the separately considered psyche itself. Apperceived in this "natural" manner, I and all other men are themes of sciences that are Objective, or positive, in the usual sense: biology, anthropology, and also (as included in these) *psychology*. The psychic life that psychology talks about has in fact always been, and still is, meant as psychic life in the world. Obviously the same is true also of one's own psychic life, which is grasped and considered in *purely internal experience*. But phenomenological epoché (which the course of our purified Cartesian meditations demands of him who is philosophizing) inhibits acceptance of the Objective world as existent, and thereby excludes this world completely from the field of judgment. In so doing, it likewise inhibits acceptance of any Objectively apperceived facts, including those of internal experience. Consequently for me, the meditating Ego who, standing / and remaining in the attitude ⟨65⟩

---

[1] The word *unberührt* (untouched) crossed out, but nothing put in its place.

[2] The word *verbleibende* (remaining) crossed out, but nothing put in its place.

[3] Author's marginal note: Kant and all his convictions relating to Ego-transcendent apperceptions, and likewise the convictions of all others, are parenthesized.

of epoché, posits exclusively himself as the *acceptance-basis* of all Objective acceptances and bases [*als Geltungsgrund aller objektiven Geltungen und Gründe*], there is no psychological Ego and there are no psychic phenomena in the sense proper to psychology, i.e., as components of psychophysical men.

By phenomenological epoché I reduce my natural human Ego and my psychic life — the realm of my *psychological self-experience* — to my transcendental-phenomenological Ego, the realm of *transcendental-phenomenological self-experience*. The Objective world, the world that exists for me, that always has and always will exist for me, the only world that ever can exist for me — this world, with all its Objects, I said, derives its whole sense and its existential status, which it has for me, from me myself, *from me as the transcendental Ego*, the Ego who comes to the fore only with transcendental-phenomenological epoché.

This concept of the transcendental and its correlate, the concept of the transcendent, must be derived exclusively from *our* philosophically meditative situation. The following should be noted in this connexion: Just as the reduced Ego is not a piece of the world, so, conversely, neither the world nor any worldly Object is a piece of my Ego, to be found in my conscious life as a really inherent part of it, as a complex of data of sensation or a complex of acts. This *"transcendence"* is part of the intrinsic sense of anything worldly, *despite* the fact that anything worldly necessarily acquires all the sense determining it, along with its existential status, exclusively from my experiencing, my objectivating, thinking, valuing, or doing, at particular times — notably the status of an evidently valid being is one it can acquire only from my own evidences, my grounding acts. If this "transcendence", which consists in being non-really included, is part of the intrinsic sense of the world, then, by way of contrast, the Ego himself, who bears within him the world as an accepted sense and who, in turn, is necessarily presupposed by this sense, is legitimately called *transcendental*, in the phenomenological sense. Accordingly the philosophical problems arising from this correlation are called transcendental-philosophical.

THE FIELD OF TRANSCENDENTAL EXPERIENCE LAID OPEN
IN RESPECT OF ITS UNIVERSAL STRUCTURES

§ 12. *The idea of a transcendental grounding of knowledge.*

Our meditations now require a further development, without which what has already been discovered cannot yield the right profit. As one who is meditating in the Cartesian manner, what can I do with the transcendental ego philosophically? Certainly his being is, for me, prior in the order of knowledge to all Objective being: In a certain sense he is the underlying basis on which all Objective cognition takes place. But can this priority rightly signify that the transcendental ego is, in the usual sense, the knowledge-basis on which all Objective knowledge is grounded? Not that we intend to abandon the great Cartesian thought of attempting to find in transcendental subjectivity the deepest grounding of all sciences and even of the being of an Objective world. If we were to abandon that thought, we should not be following Cartesian paths of meditation at all; our divergencies would be more than modifications prompted by criticism. But perhaps, with the Cartesian discovery of the transcendental ego, *a new idea of the grounding of knowledge* also becomes disclosed: the idea of it as a transcendental grounding. And indeed, instead of attempting to use *ego cogito* as an apodictically evident premise for arguments supposedly implying a transcendent subjectivity, we shall direct our attention to the fact that phenomenological epoché lays open (to me, the meditating philosopher) *an infinite realm of being of a new kind,* as the sphere of a new kind of experience: transcendental experience.[1] When we take it into consideration that, for each kind of actual experience and for each of its universal variant modes (perception, retention, recollection, etc.), there is a corresponding pure phantasy, an "as-if experience" with parallel modes (as-if

---

[1] Author's marginal note: And where there is a new experience, a new science must arise.

perception, as-if retention, as-if recollection, etc.), we surmise
that there is also an apriori science, which confines itself to the
realm of pure possibility (pure imaginableness) and, instead of
judging about actualities of transcendental being, judges about
<its > apriori possibilities and thus at the same time prescribes
rules a priori for actualities.[1] /

<67 >   But admittedly, when we let our thoughts hasten on in this
manner, to the conception of a phenomenological science destined
to become *philosophy*, we immediately run into the already-
mentioned difficulties raised by the fundamental methodological
demand for an apodictic evidence of the ego. For, as we have
already seen,[2] no matter how absolute the apodictic evidence
of the ego's existence may be for him, still it is not necessarily
evidence for the existence of the manifold data of transcendental
experience. On the other hand, though the *cogitationes* given to
me, in the attitude that effects transcendental reduction, —
given as perceived, recollected, or otherwise experience *cogitationes* — must not yet be declared absolutely indubitable with
respect to their present or past existence, still it may be possible
to show that the absolute evidence of the *ego sum* does, after all,
necessarily extend into those manifolds of self-experience in
which the ego's *transcendental life* and *habitual properties* are
given, even if there are limits that define the range of these
evidences (the evidences of recollection, retention, etc.). More
precisely stated: The bare identity of the "I am" is not the only
thing given as indubitable in transcendental self-experience.
Rather there extends through all the particular data of actual
and possible self-experience — even though they are not absolutely indubitable in respect of single details — a *universal
apodictically experienceable structure* of the Ego (for example, the
immanent temporal form belonging to the stream of subjective
processes). Perhaps it can also be shown, as something dependent
on that structure, and indeed as part of it, that the Ego is

---

[1] Author's later note: Ego [*Ich*] and habitualities are introduced for the first time
in the Fourth Meditation [§§ 31 f.]. Consideration must be given to whether that is
not too late. "Monad" [§ 33]. The concept of transcendental genesis [§ 34]? Introduction of the eidetic mode of observation [§ 34]. Why not before, at the very beginning of the Fourth Meditation or even earlier?

[2] The phrase, "as we have already seen," supplied in accordance with Typescript
C and the French translation.

apodictically predelineated, for himself, as a concrete Ego existing
with an individual content made up of subjective processes,
abilities, and dispositions — horizonally predelineated as an
experienceable object, accessible to a possible self-experience
that can be perfected, and perhaps enriched, without limit.

§ 13. *Necessity of at first excluding problems relating to the range
covered by transcendental knowledge.*

Actual demonstration that such is the case would be a great
task, *the task of a criticism of transcendental self-experience* with
respect to its / particular interwoven forms and the total effect   ‹68›
produced by the universal tissue of such forms. Obviously that
task would belong to a higher stage, since it would presuppose
that, first of all, we had followed the harmonious course of
transcendental experiencing as it functions in a certain naïve
manner, that we had made inquiries about its data and described
them in respect of their universal properties.

The broadening of the Cartesian meditations, which was just
now effected, will motivate our further procedure, as we aim at
a philosophy in the Cartesian sense already described. We see
in advance that the scientific efforts for which we found the
collective name, *transcendental phenomenology*, must proceed in
two stages.

In the *first* stage the *realm accessible to transcendental self-
experience* (a tremendous realm, as we soon discover) must be
explored — and, at first, *with simple devotion to the evidence inherent in the harmonious flow of such experience*, while questions
pertaining to an ultimate criticism, intent on apodictic principles
governing the range of evidence, are set aside. In this stage
accordingly — a stage that is *not yet philosophical in the full sense*
— we proceed like the natural scientist in his devotion to the
evidence in which Nature is experienced, while for him, as an
investigator of Nature, questions pertaining to a radical criticism
of experience remain altogether outside the field of inquiry.

The *second* stage of phenomenological research would be
precisely the *criticism of transcendental experience* and then the
criticism of *all transcendental cognition*.

A *science whose peculiar nature is unprecedented* comes into our field of vision: a science of concrete transcendental subjectivity, as given in actual and possible transcendental experience, a science that forms the *extremest contrast to sciences in the hitherto accepted sense*, positive, *"Objective"* sciences. Also among the Objective sciences there is indeed a science of subjectivity; but it is precisely the science of Objective subjectivity, the subjectivity of men and other animals, a subjectivity that is <69> part of the world. / Now, however, we are envisaging a science that is, so to speak, absolutely subjective, whose thematic object exists whether or not the world exists. But more than this. Apparently my (the philosophizer's) transcendental ego is, and must be, not only its initial but its sole theme. Without doubt the sense of the transcendental reduction implies that, at the beginning, this science can posit nothing but the ego and what is included in the ego himself, with a horizon of undetermined determinability [1]. Without doubt [it must at first parenthesize the distinction (evinced within the ego) between "me myself" with my life, my appearances, my acquired certainties of being, my abiding interests, etc., and others with their lives, their appearances, etc.; and thus, in a certain sense,] [2] it begins accordingly as a pure egology and as a science that apparently condemns us to a solipsism, albeit a transcendental solipsism. As yet it is quite impossible to foresee how, for me in the attitude of reduction, other egos — not as mere wordly phenomena but as other transcendental egos — can become positable as existing and thus become equally legitimate themes of a phenomenological egology.

As beginning philosophers we must not let ourselves be frightened by such considerations. Perhaps reduction to the transcendental ego only *seems* to entail a *permanently* solipsistic science; whereas the consequential elaboration of this science, in accordance with its own sense, leads over to a phenomenology of transcendental intersubjectivity and, by means of this, to a universal transcendental philosophy. As a matter of fact, we shall see that, in a certain manner, a transcendental solipsism is only a subordinate stage philosophically; though, as such, it

---

[1] Reading with Typescript C and the French translation. According to the published text: "with the noetic-noematic content".
[2] Inserted later.

must first be delimited for purposes of method, in order that the problems of transcendental intersubjectivity, as problems belonging to a higher level, may be correctly stated and attacked.[1] But, at this point in our meditations, we can make no definite decision about this matter; nor can the advance indications given here reveal their full significance before we have carried our meditations further.

At all events, a fundamentally essential deviation from the Cartesian course has been definitely indicated and will henceforth be decisive for all our meditating. Unlike Descartes, we shall plunge into *the task of laying open the infinite field of transcendental experience*. The Cartesian evidence — the evidence of the proposition, *ego cogito, ego sum* — remained barren because Descartes neglected, / not only to clarify the pure sense of the method of ‹70› transcendental epoché, but also to direct his attention to the fact that the ego can explicate himself *ad infinitum* and systematically, by means of transcendental experience, and therefore lies ready as a possible *field of work*. This field is completely unique and separate, since it indeed relates likewise to all the world and all the Objective sciences, yet does not presuppose acceptance of their existence, and since thereby it is separated from all these sciences, yet does not in any manner adjoin them.

§ 14. *The stream of* cogitationes. Cogito *and* cogitatum.

We now shift the weight of transcendental evidence of the *ego cogito* (this word taken in the broadest Cartesian sense) from the identical ego to the manifold *cogitationes*, the flowing conscious life in which the identical Ego (mine, the meditator's) lives — no matter what may define these expressions more particularly. (Meanwhile we understand questions about the range of the apodicticity of this evidence to be set aside.) To his conscious life — for example, his sensuously perceiving and imagining life, or his asserting, valuing, or willing life — the Ego can at any time direct his reflective regard; he can contemplate it and, in respect of its contents, explicate and describe it.

It would be much too great a mistake, if one said that to

[1] The last sentence of the preceding paragraph and this paragraph, as far as here, marked emphatically for deletion.

follow this line of research is nothing else than to make *psychological descriptions* based on purely internal experience, experience of one's own conscious life, and that naturally, to keep such descriptions pure, one must disregard everything psychophysical. A great mistake, because a *purely descriptive psychology of consciousness* (though its true method has become understandable and available only by virtue of the new phenomenology) is *not itself transcendental phenomenology* as we have defined the latter, in terms of the transcendental phenomenological reduction. To be sure, pure psychology of consciousness is a *precise parallel* to transcendental phenomenology of consciousness. Nevertheless the two must at first be kept strictly separate, since failure to distinguish them, which is characteristic of *transcendental psychologism*, makes a genuine philosophy impossible. We have ‹71› here one of those seemingly trivial nuances / that make a decisive difference between right and wrong paths of philosophy. It must be continually borne in mind that all transcendental-phenomenological research is inseparable from undeviating observance of the transcendental reduction, which must not be confounded with the abstractive restricting of anthropological research to purely psychic life. Accordingly the difference between the sense of a psychological, and that of a transcendental-phenomenological, exploration of consciousness is immeasurably profound, though the contents to be described on the one hand and on the other can correspond. In the one case we have data belonging to the world, which is presupposed as existing — that is to say, data taken as psychic components of a man. In the other case the parallel data, with their like contents, are not taken in this manner, because the whole world, when one is in the phenomenological attitude, is not accepted as actuality, but only as an actuality-phenomenon.

If this psychologistic confusion is avoided, there remains another point of decisive importance (which moreover, with a corresponding change of attitude, is decisive also, in the realm of natural experience, for a genuine *psychology* of consciousness). It must not be overlooked that epoché with respect to all worldly being does not at all change the fact that the manifold *cogitationes* relating to what is worldly bear this relation *within themselves*, that, e.g., the perception of this table still is, as it was before, precisely a perception of this table. In this manner, without exception, every conscious process is, in itself, consciousness *of* such and such, regardless of what the rightful actuality-status of this objective such-and-such may be, and regardless of the circumstance that I, as standing in the transcendental attitude, abstain from acceptance of this object as well as from all my other natural acceptances. The transcendental heading, *ego cogito*, must therefore be broadened by adding one more member. Each *cogito*, each conscious process, we may also say, *"means"* something or other and bears in itself, in this manner peculiar to the *meant*, its particular *cogitatum*. Each does this, moreover, in its own fashion. The house-perception means a house — more precisely, as this individual house — and means it in the fashion peculiar to perception; a house-memory means a house in the fashion peculiar to memory; a house-phantasy, in the fashion peculiar to phantasy. A predicative judging about a house, which perhaps is "there" perceptually, means it in just the fashion peculiar to judging; a / valuing that supervenes <72> means it in yet another fashion; and so forth. Conscious processes are also called *intentional*; but then the word intentionality signifies nothing else than this universal fundamental property of consciousness: to be consciousness *of* something; as a *cogito*, to bear within itself its *cogitatum*.[1]

§ 15. *Natural and transcendental reflection.*

For the sake of further clarification, however, it should be added that we must distinguish *"straightforwardly" executed* grasping perceiving, remembering, predicating, valuing, purposing, etc., from the *reflections* by means of which alone, as grasping acts belonging to a new level, the straightforward acts become accessible to us. Perceiving straightforwardly, we grasp, for example, the house and not the perceiving. Only in reflection do we *"direct"* ourselves to the perceiving itself and to its perceptual directedness to the house. In the *"natural reflection"* of everyday life, also however in that of psychological science (that is, in psychological experience of our own psychic

[1] Author's marginal note: This needs supplementations. Start with intentionality in the pregnant sense, that of directing oneself to something; and so forth.

processes), we stand on the footing of the world already given as
existing — as when, in everyday life, we assert: "I see a house
there" or "I remember having heard this melody". In *transcendental-phenomenological reflection* we deliver ourselves from this
footing, by universal epoché with respect to the being or non-
being of the world. The experience as thus modified, the *transcendental experience*, consists then, we can say, in our *looking at* and
describing the particular transcendentally reduced *cogito*, but
without participating, as reflective subjects, in the natural
existence-positing that the originally straightforward perception
(or other *cogito*) contains or that the Ego, as immersing himself
straightforwardly in the world, actually executed. Therewith,
to be sure, an essentially changed subjective process takes the
place of the original one; accordingly it must be said that this
reflection *alters* the original subjective process. But that is true
of every reflection, including natural reflection. Natural reflection alters the previously naïve subjective process quite
essentially; this process loses its original mode, "straightforward",
by the very fact that reflection makes an object out of what was
previously a subjective process but not objective. The proper
task of reflection, however, is not to repeat the original process,
<73> / but to consider it and explicate what can be found in it. Natu-
rally the transition to this considering yields a new intentional
process, which, with its peculiarity of "relating back to the
earlier process", is awareness, and perhaps evident awareness,
of just that earlier process itself, and not some other. Precisely
thereby an experiential knowing (which at first is descriptive)
becomes possible, that experiential knowing [*Erfahrungswissen*]
to which we owe all conceivable cognizance [*Kenntnis*] and
cognition [*Erkenntnis*] of our intentional living. This continues
to hold, then, for transcendental-phenomenological reflection.
The reflecting Ego's non-participation in the "positing" (believing, taking a position as to being) that is part of the
straightforward house-perception in no wise alters the fact that
his *reflecting* experiencing is precisely an *experiencing* experiencing of the house-perception with all its moments, which belonged to it before and are continuing to take shape. And among
these, in our example, are the moments of the perceiving itself,
as the flowing subjective process, and the moments of the per-

ceived "house", purely as perceived. There is lacking neither, on the one side, the existence-positing (perceptual belief) in the mode of certainty, which is part of — normal — perceiving, nor, on the other side (that of the appearing house), the character of simple "factual existence". The non-participating, the abstaining, of the Ego who has the phenomenological attitude is *his* affair, not that of the perceiving he considers reflectively, nor that of the naturally perceiving Ego. We may add that it is itself accessible to an appropriate reflection; and only by means of this do we know anything about it.

We can describe the situation also on the following manner. If the Ego, as naturally immersed in the world, experiencingly and otherwise, is called *"interested" in the world*, then the phenomenologically altered — and, as so altered, continually maintained — attitude consists in a *splitting of the Ego:* in that the phenomenological Ego establishes himself as *"disinterested onlooker"*, above the naïvely interested Ego. That this takes place is then itself accessible by means of a new reflection, which, as transcendental, likewise demands the very same attitude of looking on *"disinterestedly"* — the Ego's sole remaining interest being to see and to describe adequately what he sees, purely as seen, as what is seen and seen in such and such a manner.

Thus all occurences of the life turned toward the world, with all their simple and founded positings of being and with the correlative modes of being (such as certainly existing, / being <74> possible, being probable, also being beautiful and being good, being useful, etc.), pure of all accompanying and expectant meanings on the observer's part, become accessible to description. Only in this purity, indeed, can they become themes of a universal *criticism of consciousness*, such as our aiming at a philosophy necessarily demands. We recall the radicalness of the Cartesian idea of philosophy, as the idea of the all-embracing science, grounded to the utmost and apodictically. This idea demands an absolute universal criticism, which, for its part, by abstention from all positions that already give anything existent, must first create for itself a *universe of absolute freedom from prejudice*. The universality of transcendental experience and description does this by inhibiting the universal "prejudice" of world-experience, which hiddenly pervades all naturalness (the belief in the world, which pervades naturalness thoroughly and continuously), and then — within the sphere that remains unaffected, the absolute sphere of egological being, as the sphere of meanings reduced to an unalloyed freedom from prejudice — striving for a universal description. This description is then called on to be the foundation for a radical and universal criticism. Naturally everything depends on strictly preserving the absolute "unprejudicedness" of the description and thereby satisfying the principle of pure evidence, which we laid down in advance. That signifies restriction to the pure data of transcendental reflection, which therefore must be taken precisely as they are given in simple evidence, purely "intuitively", and always kept free from all interpretations that read into them more than is genuinely seen.

If we follow this methodological principle in the case of the dual topic, *cogito — cogitatum (qua cogitatum)*, there become opened to us, first of all, the general descriptions to be made, always on the basis of particular *cogitationes*, with regard to each of the two correlative sides. Accordingly, on the one hand, descriptions of the intentional object as such, with regard to the determinations attributed to it in the modes of consciousness concerned, attributed furthermore with corresponding modalities, which stand out when attention is directed to them [1]. (For example: the "modalities of being", like certainly being, possibly or presumably being, etc.; or the "subjective"- temporal modes, being present, past, or future.) This line of description is called *noematic*. Its counterpart is *noetic* description, which concerns the modes of the *cogito* / itself, the modes of consciousness (for example: perception, recollection, retention), with the modal differences inherent in them (for example: differences in clarity and distinctness).

‹75›

We now understand that, by our universal epoché with respect to the being or non-being of the world, we have not simply lost the world for phenomenology; we retain it, after all, *qua cogitatum*. And not only with respect to the *particular* realities that are meant (and *as* they are meant) in some set or other of separate acts of consciousness — or, stated more distinctly: that are meant selectively. For indeed their particularity is particularity

[1] Translator's note: In the text the pronoun is ambiguous.

within a unitary *universe*, which, even when we are directed to
and grasping the particular, goes on "appearing" unitarily. In
other words, there is always co-awareness of it, in the unity of a
consciousness that can itself become a grasping consciousness,
and often enough does. This consciousness is awareness of the
world-whole in its own peculiar form, that of spatiotemporal
endlessness. Throughout every change in consciousness the universe — changeable in its experienced (and otherwise selectively
meant) particulars, but still the one and only universe — remains
as the existing background of our whole natural life. Thus, when
phenomenological reduction is consistently executed, there is
left us, on the noetic side, the openly endless life of pure consciousness and, as its correlate on the noematic side, the meant world,
purely as meant. Accordingly, not only in respect of particulars
but also *universally*, the phenomenologically meditating Ego can
become the "non-participant onlooker" at himself — including
furthermore every Objectivity that "is" for him, and as it is for
him. Obviously it can be said that, as an Ego in the natural
attitude, I am likewise and at all times a transcendental Ego,
but that I know about this only by executing phenomenological
reduction. Only by virtue of this new attitude do I see that all
the world, and therefore whatever exists naturally, exists for
me only as accepted by me, with the sense it has for me at the
time — that it exists for me only as *cogitatum* of my changing
and, while changing, interconnected *cogitationes*; and I now
accept it solely as that. Consequently I, the transcendental phenomenologist, have *objects* (singly or in universal complexes) as
a theme for my universal descriptions: *solely as the intentional
correlates of modes of consciousness of them.* /

§ 16. *Digression: Necessary beginning of both transcendental and* <76>
      "purely psychological" reflection with the ego cogito.

According to this account, the *ego cogito* of the transcendental
ego, in the universality of his life, indicates an openly infinite
multiplicity of particular concrete subjective processes, the uncovering and descriptive apprehension of which indicates, in
turn, a first great domain of problems. Those processes are to
be uncovered and described in respect of their varying (noetic
and noematic) structures; likewise, on the other hand, in respect

of their modes of "combination" — at the highest level, in the
unity of the concrete ego himself. The ego, naturally, is concrete
only in the openly endless universality of his connectedly unitary
intentional life and of the correlates involved in it as *cogitata* —
correlates that, for their part, are united into integral universalities and include, in their number, the appearing world as
appearing. The concrete ego himself is the universal theme of
the description. Or, stated more distinctly: I, the meditating
phenomenologist, set myself the all-embracing task of *uncovering
myself*, in my full concreteness — that is, with all the intentional
correlates that are included therein. As already mentioned, the
parallel to this transcendental uncovering is the psychological
uncovering of myself, i.e., my purely psychic being and, first of
all, my psychic life, apperceived in the natural manner, namely
as a component of my psychophysical (animal) reality and thus
as a component of the world I naturally accept.

Manifestly a transcendental-descriptive egology, and likewise
a descriptive *"purely inner psychology"* actually derived quite
exclusively from internal experience (a psychology that, as the
fundamental psychological discipline, must be developed), can
start with nothing other than the *ego cogito*. What with the
failure of all modern attempts to distinguish between a psychological and a philosophical theory of consciousness, this remark
is of the greatest importance. Access to both theories is barred,
if one is misled by the still all-prevailing tradition of sensualism
and starts with a theory of sensation. To do so involves the
following: In advance, as though this were obviously correct,
one misinterprets conscious life as a complex of data of "external" and (at best) "internal sensuousness"; then one lets /
‹77› form-qualities take care of combining such data into wholes. To
get rid of "atomism", one adds the theory that the forms or
configurations are founded on these data necessarily and the
wholes are therefore prior in themselves to the parts. But, when
descriptive theory of consciousness begins radically, it has before
it no such data and wholes, except perhaps as prejudices. Its
beginning is the pure — and, so to speak, still dumb — psychological [1] experience, which now must be made to utter its own

---

[1] Reading *"psychologische"* instead of *"psychische"* (psychic), as in both the
published text and typescript C.

sense with no adulteration. The truly first utterance, however, is the Cartesian utterance of the *ego cogito* — for example: "I perceive — this house" or "I remember — a certain commotion in the street". And the first descriptive generality is the separation of *cogito* and *cogitatum qua cogitatum*. In what cases, and in what different significations of the phrase, data of sensation can then perhaps be tendered legitimately as components: that is ‹a problem whose solution is› a special result, to be produced by a work of uncovering and describing — from which the traditional theory of consciousness has completely exempted itself, to its own detriment. Since it was not clear about the fundamental essentials of method, it entirely missed not only the tremendous theme of describing *cogitata qua cogitata* but also the proper sense and particular tasks belonging to a description of *cogitationes* themselves, as modes of consciousness.

§ 17. *The two-sidedness of inquiry into consciousness as an investigation of correlatives. Lines of description. Synthesis as the primal form belonging to consciousness.*

On the other hand, if the beginning and the direction in which our tasks lie are clear from the first, they provide us, in our transcendental attitude, with important *thoughts to guide the attack on further problems*. Inquiry into consciousness concerns *two sides* (for the present we are leaving out of consideration the question of the identical Ego); they can be characterized descriptively as *belonging together inseparably*. The sort of combination uniting consciousness with consciousness can be characterized as *synthesis*, a mode of combination exclusively peculiar to consciousness. For example, if I take the perceiving of this die as the theme for my description, I see in pure reflection that "this" die is given continuously as an objective unity in a multiform and changeable multiplicity of manners of appearing, which belong determinately to it. These, in their temporal flow, are not an incoherent sequence of / subjective processes. Rather ‹78› they flow away in the unity of a synthesis, such that in them "one and the same" is intended as appearing. The one identical die appears, now in "near appearances", now in "far appearances": in the changing modes of the Here and There, over against an always co-intended, though perhaps unheeded, absolute Here (in my co-appearing organism). Furthermore, each continued manner of appearance in such a mode (for example: "the die here, in the near sphere") shows itself to be, in turn, the synthetic unity pertaining to a multiplicity of manners of appearance belonging to that mode. Thus the near-thing, as "the same", appears now from this "side", now from that; and the "visual perspectives" change — also, however, the other manners of appearance (tactual, acoustic, and so forth), as we can observe by turning our attention in the right direction. Then, if we pay particular heed to any of the die's features that shows itself in the die-perception (for example: the die's shape or color, or one of its faces in particular, or the square shape or particular color of that face), the same is again the case. Always we find the feature in question as a unity belonging to a passing flow of "multiplicities". Looking straightforwardly, we have perhaps the one unchanging shape or color; in the reflective attitude, we have its manners of appearance (orientational, perspectival, and so forth), following one another in continuous sequence. Furthermore, each of these manners of appearance (for example: the shadowing forth [*Abschattung*] of the shape or color) is itself an *exhibition of* [*Darstellung von*] the shape, the color, or whatever the feature is that appears in it. Thus each passing cogito intends its cogitatum, not with an undifferentiated blankness, but as a cogito with a describable *structure of multiplicities*, a structure having a *quite definite* noetic-noematic composition, which, by virtue of its essential nature, pertains to just *this* identical cogitatum.

Parallel and (as becomes apparent in making them) extremely far-reaching descriptions can be developed in the case of any intuition — that is, not only in the case of sensuous perception, but also in the case of other modes of intuition (recollection, which makes intuited afterwards; expectation, which makes intuited beforehand). For example: the remembered physical thing also appears "in" changing sides, perspectives, and so forth. But, in order to do justice to the differences among modes of intuition (for example: to what differentiates givenness in memory / from givenness in perception), other dimensions would have to be described. One most general trait, however, is always

<79>

present in any consciousness of any sort, as consciousness of something: This something, the particular "intentional object qua intentional" in any consciousness, is there [*bewusst*] as an identical unity belonging to noetically-noematically changing modes of consciousness, whether intuitive or non-intuitive.

Once we have laid hold of the phenomenological task of describing consciousness concretely, veritable infinities of facts — never explored prior to phenomenology — become disclosed. They can all be characterized as *facts of synthetic structure*, which give noetic-noematic unity to single cogitationes, in themselves (as concrete synthetic wholes) and in relation to one another. Only elucidation of the peculiarity we call synthesis makes fruitful the exhibition of the cogito (the intentional subjective process) as consciousness-of — that is to say, Franz Brentano's significant discovery that "intentionality" is the fundamental characteristic of "psychic phenomena" — and actually lays open the method for a descriptive transcendental-philosophical theory of consciousness (and naturally also for a corresponding psychological theory).

§ 18. *Identification as the fundamental form of synthesis. The all-embracing synthesis of transcendental time.*

If we consider the *fundamental form of synthesis*, namely *identification*, we encounter it first of all as an all-ruling, *passively* flowing synthesis, in the form of the *continuous consciousness of internal time*. Every subjective process has its internal temporality. If it is a conscious process in which (as in the perception of the die) a worldly Object appears as cogitatum, then we have to distinguish the *Objective temporality that appears* (for example: the temporality of this die) from the *"internal" temporality of the appearing* (for example: that of the die-perceiving). This appearing "flows away" with its temporal extents and phases, which, for their part, are continually changing appearances *of* the one identical die. Their unity is a unity of synthesis: not merely a continuous connectedness of cogitationes (as it were, a being stuck to one another externally), but *a connectedness that makes the unity of one consciousness*, in which the unity of an intentional objectivity, as "the same" objectivity / belonging <80>

to multiple modes of appearance, becomes "*constituted*". The existence of a world and, accordingly, the existence of this die are "parenthesized" in consequence of my epoché; but the one identical, appearing die (as appearing) [1] is continuously "immanent" in the flowing consciousness, *descriptively "in" it*; as is likewise the attribute "one identical". This being-in-consciousness is a *being-in of a completely unique kind:* not a being-in-consciousness as a really intrinsic component part, but rather a being-in-it "ideally" as something *intentional*, something appearing — or, equivalantly stated, a being-in-it as its immanent "*objective sense*". The "object" of consciousness, the object as having identity "with itself" during the flowing subjective process, does not come into the process from outside; on the contrary, it is included as a sense in the subjective process itself — and thus as an "*intentional effect*" *produced by* the synthesis of consciousness.

Now the same die (the same for consciousness) can be intended in highly diverse modes of consciousness — simultaneously, or else successively in *separated* modes of consciousness — for example: in separate perceptions, recollections, expectations, valuations, and so forth. Again it is a synthesis that, as a unitary consciousness *embracing* these separated processes, gives rise to the consciousness of identity and thereby makes any knowing of identity possible.

But likewise every consciousness in which the *non-identical* is intended unitarily (every consciousness of a plurality, a relational complex, or the like) is ultimately a *synthesis* in this sense, constituting its peculiar cogitatum (the plurality, the relational complex, or whatever it is) synthetically or, as is also said here, syntactically — regardless, moreover, of whether this synthesis should be characterized as a pure passivity on the Ego's part or as his activity. Even contradictions, incompatibilities, are products of "syntheses" (to be sure, syntheses of another kind).

Synthesis, however, does not occur just in every particular conscious process, nor does it connect one particular conscious process with another only occasionally. On the contrary, as we said beforehand, the *whole of conscious life is unified synthetically*. Conscious life is therefore an all-embracing "cogito", syn-

---

[1] Supplied in accordance with Typescript C.

thetically comprising all particular conscious processes that ever become prominent, and having its all-embracing cogitatum, founded at different levels on the manifold particular cogitata. But this founding does not signify a building up in the temporal / sequence of a genesis, since indeed any imaginable particular <81> subjective process is only a prominence within a total consciousness always presupposed as unitary.[1] The all-embracing cogitatum <of reflection> is the all-embracing life itself, with its openly endless unity and wholeness. Only because it already appears as a total unity can it also be "contemplated", in the pre-eminent manner characterizing acts of paying attention and grasping, and be made the theme for an all-embracing cognition. The *fundamental form* of this universal synthesis, the form that makes all other syntheses of consciousness possible, is the all-embracing *consciousness of internal time*. The correlate of this consciousness is immanent temporality itself, in conformity with which all the life-processes belonging to the ego that can ever be found reflectively must present themselves as temporally ordered, temporally beginning and ending, simultaneous or successive, within the constant infinite horizon: immanent time. The distinction between <internal> time itself and the consciousness of <internal> time can be expressed also as that between the subjective process in internal time, or the temporal form of this process, and the *modes of its temporal appearance*, as the corresponding "multiplicities". As these modes of appearance, which make up the consciousness of internal time, are themselves "intentive components of conscious life" ["*intentionale Erlebnisse*"] and must in turn be given in reflection as temporalities, we encounter here a paradoxical fundamental property of conscious life, which seems thus to be infected with an infinite regress. The task of clarifying this fact and making it understandable presents extraordinary difficulties. Be that as it may, the fact is evident, even apodictically evident, and indicates one aspect of the ego's marvellous being-for-himself: here, in the first place, the being of his conscious life in the form of reflexive intentional relatedness to itself.

---

[1] Author's marginal note: All this requires further supplemantation, relating to the consciousness (within the ego) of intersubjective time.

§ 19. *Actuality and potentiality of intentional life.*

The multiplicity of the intentionality belonging to any cogito — to any that relates to the world, by the very fact that such a cogito not only intends something wordly but is itself intended in the consciousness of internal time — is a theme not exhausted with the consideration of cogitationes [1] as *actual* subjective processes. On the contrary, *every actuality involves its potentialities*, which are not empty possibilities, but rather possibilities <82> / intentionally predelineated in respect of content — namely, in the actual subjective process itself — and, in addition, having the character of possibilities *actualizable by the Ego*.

With that, *another fundamental trait of intentionality* is indicated. Every subjective process has a process [2] "horizon", which changes with the alteration of the nexus of consciousness to which the process belongs and with the alteration of the process itself from phase to phase of its flow — an intentional *horizon of reference* to potentialities of consciousness that belong to the process itself. For example, there belongs to every external perception its reference from the "genuinely perceived" sides of the object of perception to the sides "also meant" — not yet perceived, but only anticipated and, at first, with a non-intuitional emptiness (as the sides that are "coming" now perceptually): a continuous *protention*, which, with each phase of the perception, has a new sense. Furthermore, the perception has horizons made up of other possibilities of perception, as perceptions that we *could* have, if we *actively directed* the course of perception otherwise: if, for example, we turned our eyes that way instead of this, or if we were to step forward or to one side, and so forth. In the corresponding memory this recurs in modified form, perhaps in the consciousness that, instead of the sides then visible in fact, I could have seen others — naturally, *if* I had directed my perceptual activity in a suitably different manner. Moreover, as might have been said earlier, to every perception there always belongs a horizon of the past, as a potentiality of awakenable recollections; and to every recollection there belongs, as a horizon, the continuous intervening intentionality of possible

---

[1] In the published text, Typescript C, and the French translation: cogitata.
[2] Inserted later.

recollections (to be actualized on my initiative, actively), up to the actual Now of perception. Everywhere in this connexion an "I can and do, but I can also do otherwise than I am doing" plays its part — without detriment to the fact that this "freedom", like every other, is always open to possible hindrances.

The horizons are "predelineated" potentialities. We say also: We can *ask any horizon what "lies in it"*, we can *explicate* or unfold it, and *"uncover"* the potentialities of conscious life at a particular time. Precisely thereby we uncover the *objective sense meant implicitly* in the actual cogito, though never with more than a certain degree of foreshadowing. This sense, the *cogitatum qua cogitatum*, is never present to actual consciousness [*vorstellig*] as a finished datum; it becomes "clarified" only through explication of the given horizon and the new / horizons continu- ‹83›
ously awakened [*der stetig neu geweckten Horizonte*]. The predelineation itself, to be sure, is at all times imperfect; yet, with its *indeterminateness*, it has a *determinate structure*. For example: the die leaves open a great variety of things pertaining to the unseen faces; yet it is already "construed" in advance as a die, in particular as colored, rough, and the like, though each of these determinations always leaves further particulars open. This leaving open, prior to further determinings (which perhaps never take place), is a moment included in the given consciousness itself; it is precisely what makes up the "horizon". As contrasted with mere [1] clarification by means of anticipative "imaginings", there takes place, by means of an actually continuing perception, a *fulfilling* further determination (and perhaps determination as otherwise) — but with new horizons of openness.

Thus, as consciousness of something, every consciousness has the essential property, not just of being somehow *able to change into continually new modes of consciousness of the same object* (which, throughout the unity of synthesis, is inherent in them as an identical objective sense), but of being able to do so according to — indeed, *only according to those horizon intentionalities* [2]. The object is, so to speak, *a pole of identity*, always meant

---

[1] Reading, with Typescript C, "*blossen*" instead of "*grossen*". Cf. the French: "*simple*".

[2] Reading, with Typescript C, "*-intentionalitäten*", instead of "*-intentionalität*".

expectantly as having a sense yet to be actualized; in every moment of consciousness it is an index, pointing to a noetic intentionality that pertains to it according to its sense, an intentionality that can be asked for and explicated. All this is concretely accessible to investigation.

§ 20. *The peculiar nature of intentional analysis.*

It becomes evident that, as intentional, the analysis of consciousness is totally different from analysis in the usual and natural sense. Conscious life, as we said once before, is not just a whole made up of "data" of consciousness and therefore "analyzable" (in an extremely broad sense, divisible) merely into its selfsufficient and non-selfsufficient *elements* — the forms of unity (the "form-qualities") being included then among the non-selfsufficient elements. To be sure, when regard is directed to certain themes, intentional "analysis" does lead *also* to such divisions, and to that extent the word can still serve in the original sense; but everywhere its peculiar attainment (as "intentional") is an uncovering of the *potentialities "implicit"* in actualities of consciousness — an uncovering that brings about, ‹84› on the noematic side, an / "explication" or "unfolding", a "becoming distinct" and perhaps a "clearing" of what is consciously meant (the objective sense) and, correlatively, an explication of the potential intentional processes themselves. Intentional analysis is guided by the fundamental cognition that, as a consciousness, every cogito is indeed (in the broadest sense) a meaning of its meant [*Meinung seines Gemeinten*], but that, at any moment, this something meant [*dieses Vermeinte*] is more — something meant with something more — than what is meant at that moment "explicitly". In our example, each phase of perception was a mere side of "the" object, as what was perceptually meant. This *intending-beyond-itself*, which is implicit in any consciousness, must be considered an essential moment of it. That, on the other hand, this intending is, and must be, a "meaning more" of the Same becomes shown only by the evidence of a possible making distinct and, ultimately, of an intuitive uncovering, in the form of actual and possible continued perceiving or of possible recollecting, as something to be done on my initiative.

The phenomenologist, however, does not inquire with merely a naïve devotedness to the intentional object purely as such; he does not consider the intentional object only straightforwardly and explicate its meant features, its meant parts and properties. If that were all he did, the intentionality, which makes up the intuitive or non-intuitive consciousness itself and the explicative considering, would remain "anonymous". In other words: There would remain hidden the noetic multiplicities of consciousness and their synthetic unity, by virtue of which alone, and as their essentially necessary unitary doing [*ihre wesensmässige Einheitsleistung*], we have one intentional object, and always this definite one, continuously meant — have it, so to speak, before us *as* meant thus and so; likewise the hidden constitutive performances by virtue of which (if consideration then continues as explication) we find straightforwardly, as explicata of what is meant, such things as a "feature", a "property" [1] a "part", or mean these implicitly and can then discover them intuitively. When the phenomenologist explores everything objective, and whatever can be found in it, exclusively as a "correlate of consciousness", he does not consider and describe it only straightforwardly and only as *somehow* related back to the corresponding Ego and the *ego cogito* of which it is the *cogitatum*. Rather, with his reflective regard, he penetrates the anonymous "cogitative" life, he uncovers the *definite* synthetic courses of the manifold modes of consciousness and, / further back, the ⟨85⟩ modes of Ego-comportment, which make understandable the objective affair's simple meantness for the Ego, its intuitive or non-intuitive meantness. Or, stated more precisely, they make it understandable how, in itself and by virtue of its current intentional structure, consciousness makes possible and necessary the fact that such an "existing" and "thus determined" Object is intended in it, occurs in it as such a sense. Thus, in the case of perception of a spatial thing, the phenomenologist (abstracting at first from all "significance" predicates and restricting himself purely to the "res extensa") explores the manner in which the changing "sight things", and "things" of the other senses, have in themselves the character of appearances *of* this same res

---

Author's marginal note: substratum.

extensa. In the case of any spatial thing, he explores its [1] (potential and perhaps actual) changing perspectives; furthermore, with regard to its temporal modes of givenness, the modifications of its being still intended while it sinks retentionally into the past and, with respect to the Ego, the modes of his specifically own still-having and holding, the modes of attention, and so forth. It is to be noted in this connexion that phenomenological explication of the perceived as such is not restricted to that perceptual explication of it, in respect of its features, which comes about as perception continues. On the contrary, phenomenological explication makes clear what is included and only non-intuitively co-intended in the sense of the cogitatum (for example, the "other side"), by making present in phantasy the potential perceptions that would make the invisible visible. That is true of any intentional analysis. As intentional *it reaches out beyond the isolated subjective processes* that are to be analyzed. By explicating their correlative horizons, it brings the highly diverse anonymous processes into the field comprising those that function "constitutively" in relation to the objective sense of the cogitatum in question — that is to say: not only the actual but also the *potential* subjective processes, which, as such, are "implicit" and "predelineated" in the sense-producing intentionality of the actual ones and which, when discovered, have the evident character of processes that explicate the implicit sense. Thus alone can the phenomenologist make understandable to himself *how*, within the immanency of conscious life and in thus and so determined modes of consciousness belonging to this incessant flux, anything like *fixed and abiding objective unities* can become intended and, in particular, how this marvellous work of "constituting" identical objects is done *in*
‹86› *the case of each category of objects* / — that is to say: how, in the case of each category, the constitutive conscious life looks, and must look, in respect of the correlative noetic and noematic variants pertaining to the same object. The *horizon structure* belonging to every intentionality thus prescribes for phenomenological analysis and description *methods of a totally new kind*, which come into action wherever consciousness and object, wherever intending and sense, real and ideal actuality, possi-

[1] Reading, with Typescript C, "ihre" instead of "ihrer".

bility, necessity, illusion, truth, and, on the other hand, experience, judgment, evidence, and so forth, present themselves as names for transcendental problems, to be taken in hand as genuine problems concerning "subjective origins".

Mutatis mutandis the same is manifestly true in the case of a pure [1] "internal psychology" or a "purely intentional" psychology (within the realm of natural positivity) [2], which we have alluded to as the parallel to constitutional transcendental phenomenology. The only radical reform of psychology consists in the pure development of an intentional psychology. Brentano demanded it; but unfortunately he failed to recognize the fundamental sense of an intentional analysis and therefore failed to recognize the method that alone makes such a psychology possible, as the latter can gain access to its genuine and truly infinite field of problems only by that method.

At first, to be sure, the possibility of a pure phenomenology of consciousness seems highly questionable, since the realm of phenomena of consciousness is so truly the realm of a Heraclitean flux. It would in fact be hopeless to attempt to proceed here with such methods of concept and judgment formation as are standard in the Objective sciences. The attempt to determine a process of consciousness as an identical object, on the basis of experience, in the same fashion as a natural Object — ultimately then with the ideal presumption of a possible explication into identical elements, which might be apprehended by means of fixed concepts — would indeed be folly. Processes of consciousness — not merely owing to our imperfect ability to know objects of that kind, but a priori — have no ultimate elements and relationships, fit for subsumption under the idea of objects determinable by fixed concepts and therefore such that, in their case, it would be rational to set ourselves the task of an approximative determination guided by fixed concepts. In spite of that, however, the idea of an intentional analysis is legitimate, since, in the flux of intentional synthesis (which creates unity in all consciousness and which, noetically and noematically, constitutes unity of objective sense), *an essentially necessary conformity to type* prevails and *can be apprehended in strict concepts.* | <87>

[1] Supplied in accordance with Typescript C and the French translation.
[2] Supplied in accordance with Typescript C and the French translation.

§ 21. *The intentional object as "transcendental clue"*.

[1] The most universal type — within which, as a form, everything particular is included — is indicated by our first universal
scheme: *ego — cogito — cogitatum*. The most universal descriptions (made with the most extreme, with — so to speak —
formal, universality), which we have attempted in a rough
fashion concerning intentionality, concerning its peculiar synthesis, and so forth, relate to that type. In the particularization of
that type, and of its description, the *intentional object* (on the
side belonging to the *cogitatum*) plays, for easily understood
reasons, the role of "transcendental clue" to the typical infinite
multiplicities of possible *cogitationes* that, in a possible synthesis,
bear the intentional object within them (in the manner peculiar
to consciousness) as the same meant object. Necessarily the point
of departure is the object given "straightforwardly" at the particular time. From it reflection goes back to the mode of
consciousness at that time and to the potential modes of
consciousness included horizonally in that mode, then to those
in which the object might be otherwise intended as the same,
within the unity (ultimately) of a possible conscious life, all the
possibilities of which are included in the "ego". If we continue
to limit ourselves to the most extreme universality, to *formal
universality*, if we think of just any object (with an unrestrictedly
optional content) as *cogitatum*, and take it in this universality as
our clue, we find that the multiplicity of possible modes of
consciousness of the Same — the formal type that all these ex-
emplify — is subdivided into a number of sharply differentiated
particular types. For example, possible perception, retention,
recollection, expectation, intending as something symbolized,
intuitive representation by analogy, are such types of intentionality, which pertain to *any conceivable object*, as do their
types of synthetic combination. All these types become further
particularized in their whole noetic-noematic composition as
soon as we particularize the empty universality of the intentional
object. The particularization may at first be formal-logical
(formal-ontological) — that is to say: modes of the Anything

---

[1] Author's note opposite first line of text: Intentional modifications of the cogito
— memories and empathies.

Whatever, such as single object, and ultimately individual object, universal, plurality, whole, predicatively formed state (or complex) of affairs, relational complex, and so forth. Here the radical difference between *objectivities that are real* (in a broad sense) and *categorial objectivities* also presents itself. The latter point back to an origin from "operations", from a step-by-step generative-constructive / activity of the ego: the former, to an ⟨88⟩ origin as effects of a merely passive (in any case, not an ⟨actively⟩ generative) synthesis. On the other hand, we have the *material-ontological* particularizations, starting from the concept of the real concrete individual, which is differentiated into its real regions — for example: (mere) spatial thing, animate being, and so forth — and entails corresponding particularizations of the relevant formal-logical modifications (real property, real plurality, real relational complex, and the rest).

Each type brought out by these clues is to be asked about its noetic-noematic structure, is to be systematically explicated and established in respect of those modes of intentional flux that pertain to it, and in respect of their horizons and the intentional processes implicit in their horizons, and so forth. If one keeps no matter what object fixed in its form or category and maintains continuous evidence of its identity throughout the change in modes of consciousness of it, one sees that, no matter how fluid these may be, and no matter how inapprehensible as having ultimate elements, still they are by no means variable without restriction. They are always restricted to a set of *structural types*, which is "invariable", inviolably the same: as long as the objectivity remains intended as *this* one and as of this kind, and as long as, throughout the change in modes of consciousness, evidence of objective identity can persist.

To explicate systematically just this set of structural types is the *task of transcendental theory*, which, if it restricts itself to an objective universality as its clue, is called theory of the transcendental constitution of any object whatever, as an object of the form or category (highest of all, the region) in question. Thus arise — first of all, as separate — many different transcendental theories: a theory of perception and the other types of intuition, a theory of intending objects as symbolized, a theory of judgment, a theory of volition, and so forth. They become united, however, in view of the more comprehensive synthetic complexes; they belong together functionally, and thus make up the *formally universal* constitutional theory of *any object whatever* or of an open horizon of possible *objects of any sort*, as objects of possible consciousness.

‹89›   Furthermore, transcendental / theories of constitution arise that, as non-formal, relate to any spatial things whatever (singly and in the all-embracing nexus of a Nature), to any psychophysical beings, to human beings as such, to their self-comportment toward their natural and otherwise determined surrounding world, to any social communities, any cultural objects, and ultimately to any Objective world whatever — purely as a world intended in possible consciousness and, transcendentally, as a world constituted (in the manner peculiar to consciousness) purely within the transcendental ego. All of that, naturally, with consistently exercised transcendental epoché, from which all these theories derive a transcendental sense.[1]

Yet it must not be overlooked that types of real and ideal objects intended as *"Objective"* are not the only clues for consti-

---

[1] At about this point Husserl inserted a page of text, which may be translated as follows.

‹238›   Yet I had to begin with myself, the Ego given in experience of myself as a man. After all, I could exercise reduction only by starting out from myself; and therefore I arrived only at the ego who has, as his worldly counterpart, his own psyche. My own human psyche, therefore, I can make evident as a manifestation of the absolute: What are others, what is the world, for me? — Constituted phenomena, merely something produced within me. Never can I reach the point of ascribing being in the absolute sense to others, any more than to the physical things of Nature, which exist only as transcendentally produced affairs. Meditations I–IV concern a first path, along which it becomes visible in a very general manner that, for the ego of the transcendental reduction, all that exists is and must be a constituted product. But must it not be said likewise that all that exists for me as a man must be constituted within me, in the manner peculiar to consciousness — including my own humanness? How is the latter proposition related to the former? Conscious life is likewise constituted necessarily as human in the constituted world, and as a human conscious life in which the world is intended, psychically constituted, and so forth.

‹239›   The all-embracing constitution of the world within the ego is outlined as a problem only / as far as the theory of clues — as far as the consideration of the world (that is to say: the ontological consideration thereof, as transformed into a constitutional-ontological consideration). Somewhere in that context, naturally, the problem *man* must present itself? But what is the proper order?

The first procedure in Meditations I–IV is to awaken the guiding thought: The world is a meaning, an accepted sense. When we go back to the ego, we can explicate the founding and founded strata with which that sense is built op [*den Fundierungsaufbau*], we can reach the absolute being and process in which the being of the world shows its ultimate truth and in which the ultimate problems of being reveal themselves — bringing into the thematic field all the disguises that unphilosophical naiveté cannot penetrate [*alle Verhüllungen der unphilosophischen Naivität*].

tutional investigations — that is, when we inquire into the universal types of possible modes of consciousness of objects. The types of *merely subjective objects*, such as all immanent subjective processes themselves, are likewise clues, since, as objects of the consciousness of internal time, they have (singly and universally) their "constitution".

Everywhere problems of *particular, separately considered* kinds of objects and *problems of universality* become distinguishable. The latter concern the ego in the universality of his being and living and in his relation to the corresponding universality of his objective correlates. If we take the unitary Objective world as a transcendental clue, it leads back to the synthesis of Objective perceptions and other Objective intuitions, which extends throughout the unity of life as a whole, and is such that the world is at all times intended — and can become thematic — as a unit. Consequently the world is a universal problem of egology, as is likewise the whole of conscious life, in its immanent temporality, when we direct our regard to the purely immanent.

§ 22. *The idea of the universal unity comprising all objects, and the task of clarifying it constitutionally.*

Types of objects — viewed with the attitude established by phenomenological reduction, purely as cogitata, and not construed with the "prejudices" involved in a set of scientific concepts accepted in advance — were found to be clues for transcendental investigations, which belong together on account of their themes. The fact is that the constituting multiplicities of consciousness — those actually or possibly combined to make the unity of an identifying synthesis — are not accidental but, as regards the possibility / of such a synthesis, *belong together for* ‹90› *essential reasons.* Accordingly they are governed by *principles,* thanks to which our phenomenological investigations do not get lost in disconnected descriptions but are essentially organized. Any "Objective" object, *any object whatever* (even an immanent one), points to *a structure, within the transcendental ego, that is governed by a rule.* As something the ego objectivates, something of which he is conscious in any manner, the object indicates forthwith a universal rule governing *possible* other consciousnesses of it as identical — possible, as exemplifying essentially predelineated types. And naturally the same is true of any "imaginable" object, anything conceivable as something intended. Transcendental subjectivity is not a chaos of intentional processes. Moreover, it is not a chaos of types of constitution, each organized in itself by its relation to a kind or a form of intentional objects. In other words: The *allness* of objects and types of objects conceivable for me — transcendentally speaking: for me as transcendental ego — is no chaos; and correlatively the allness of the types of the infinite multiplicities, the types corresponding to types of objects, is not a chaos either: noetically and noematically those multiplicities always belong together, in respect of their possible synthesis.

That indicates in advance a *universal constitutive synthesis*, in which all syntheses function together in a definitely ordered manner and in which therefore all actual and possible objectivities (as actual and possible for the transcendental ego), and correlatively all actual and possible modes of consciousness of them, are embraced. Furthermore we can say that an enormous task is foreshadowed, which is that of transcendental phenomenology as a whole: the task of *carrying out all phenomenological investigations* within the unity of a systematic and all-embracing order by following, as our mobile clue, a system to be found out level by level, the system namely of all objects of possible consciousness, including the system of their formal and material categories — the task, I say, of carrying out such investigations as *corresponding constitutional investigations*, one based upon another, and all of them interconnected, in a strictly systematic fashion.

But we speak more correctly if we say that here it is a matter of an infinite *regulative idea*, that the evidently presupposable
‹91› system of possible objects of possible / consciousness is itself an anticipative idea (not however an invention, an "as if"), and that, as regards practice, it equips us with the principle for combining any relatively closed constitutional theory with any other: by an incessant uncovering of horizons — not only those belonging to objects of consciousness internally, but also those having an external reference, namely to essential forms of interconnexions. To be sure, even the tasks that present themselves

when we take single types of objects as restricted clues prove
to be extremely complicated and always lead to extensive disciplines when we penetrate more deeply. That is the case, for
example, with a transcendental theory of the constitution of a
spatial object (to say nothing of a Nature) as such, of psychophysical being and humanity as such, culture as such.

THIRD MEDITATION

CONSTITUTIONAL PROBLEMS. TRUTH AND ACTUALITY

§ 23. *A more pregnant concept of constitution, under the titles "reason" and "unreason".*

Phenomenological constitution has been for us, up to now, constitution of any intentional object whatever. It has embraced the full breadth of the topic, cogito — cogitatum. We shall now proceed to differentiate this breadth structurally, and to prepare for a *more pregnant concept of constitution*. It has not mattered up to now, whether the objects in question were truly existent or non-existent, or whether they were possible or impossible. These differences are not perchance excluded from the field of inquiry by abstaining from decision about the being or non-being of the world (and, consequently, of other already-given objectivities). On the contrary, under the broadly understood titles, *reason and unreason*, as correlative titles for being and non-being, they are an all-embracing theme for phenomenology. By epoché we effect a reduction to our pure meaning (cogito) and to the meant, purely as meant. The predicates *being and non-being*, and their modal variants, relate to the latter — accordingly, not to objects simpliciter but to the *objective sense*. |

‹92› The predicates *truth (correctness) and falsity*, albeit in a most extremely broad sense, relate to the former, to the particular *meaning or intending*. These predicates are not given ipso facto as phenomenological data, when the subjective meaning processes, or correlatively the meant objects as meant, are given; yet they have their "phenomenological origin". As we have said, the multiplicities of modes of consciousness that belong together synthetically and pertain to any meant object, of no matter what category, can be explored as to their phenomenological types. Among such multiplicities are included those syntheses that, with regard to the initial intending, have the typical style of verifying and, in particular, evidently verifying syntheses — or else, on the contrary, that of nullifying and evidently nullifying syntheses. When such a synthesis takes place, the meant object has, correlatively, the evident characteristic *existing*, or else the evident characteristic *non-existing* (the characteristic of annulled, of "cancelled" being). These synthetic occurences are intentionalities of a higher level, which, as acts and correlates of "reason", essentially producible by the transcendental ego, pertain (in exclusive disjunction) to all objective senses. *Reason is not an accidental de facto ability*, not a title for possible accidental matters of fact, but rather a title for an *all-embracing essentially necessary structural form belonging to all transcendental subjectivity.*

Reason refers to possibilites of verification; and verification refers ultimately to making evident and having as evident. About evidence we had to speak even at the beginning of our meditations — when, with our initial naïveté, we were still seeking the guiding lines for a method and had not yet set foot within the realm of phenomenology. It now becomes our phenomenological theme.

§ 24. *Evidence as itself-givenness and the modifications of evidence.*

In the broadest sense, evidence denotes a universal primal phenomenon of intentional life, namely — as contrasted with other consciousness-of, which is capable a priori of being "empty", expectant, indirect, non-presentive — the quite preeminent mode of consciousness that consists in the *self-appearance*, the *self-exhibiting*, the *self-giving*, of an affair, an affair-complex (or state of affairs), a universality, a value, or other objectivity, in the final mode: "itself there", "immediately intuited", / "given originaliter". For the Ego that signifies: not ‹93› aiming confusedly at something, with an empty expectant intention, but being with it itself, viewing, seeing, having insight into, it itself. Experience in the ordinary sense is a particular evidence. All evidence, we may say, is *experience in a maximally broad, and yet essentially unitary*, sense. In the case of most objects, to be sure, evidence is only an occasional occurrence in conscious life; yet it is a possibility — and, more particularly, one that can be the aim of a striving and actualizing intention

— in the case of anything meant already or meanable. Thus it points to an essential *fundamental trait of all intentional life.* Any consciousness, without exception, either is itself already characterized as evidence (that is, as giving its object originaliter) or else has an essential tendency toward conversion into givings of its object originaliter — accordingly, toward syntheses of verification, which belong essentially in the domain of the "I can". In the attitude established by transcendental reduction, we can ask any vague consciousness whether, and to what extent, while the identity of the meant object is preserved, the meant object in the mode "it itself" corresponds (or can correspond) to that consciousness; or, equivalently, how the presupposed object would have to look as "it itself" — that which, as yet, is indeterminately anticipated becoming, at the same time, more particulary determined. During the process of verification, verification can turn into its negative; instead of the meant itself, a "different" can come to the fore, and do so in the mode "it itself" — a different that wrecks the positing of what was meant, so that the previously meant, for its part, assumes the character: nullity.

Non-being is only a *modality* of simple being, of certain being (which is the primal mode) — a modality that, for certain reasons, has a pre-eminent place in logic. But evidence, in a maximally broad sense, is a concept that is correlated not only with the concepts being and non-being. It becomes modalized also in correlation with the other modal variants of simple being, such as being possible, probable, or doubtful — likewise, however, in correlation with variants that do not belong in this series but have their origin in the spheres of emotion and volition, such as being valuable and being morally good.

§ 25. *Actuality and quasi-actuality.*

<94>   All these differences moreover are bifurcated, / on account of a difference that extends throughout the whole sphere of consciousness and, correlatively, throughout all modalities of being: the difference, namely, between actuality and phantasy (as-if actuality). On this side a new universal concept of *possibility* arises, which, as mere "imaginableness" (in a phantasying, as if something were), repeats in modified form all the modes of

being, starting with simple certainty of being. It repeats them
as modes belonging to purely phantasied "non-actualities", in
contrast to the modes belonging to "actuality" (actual being,
actual being probable or doubtful, actual being not). *Correlatively, modes of consciousness* are likewise divided into those of
"positionality" and those of *"quasi-positionality"* (of the as-if,
of "phantasying" — admittedly too ambiguous an expression);
and to each of these modes there correspond both a particular
mode of evidence of its meant objects — in the appropriate
mode of being — and potentialities of making objects evident.
Here belongs what we often call *clarification.* Making clear is
always a mode of *making evident,* of laying a synthetic course
from an unclear intending to a corresponding *"prefigurative"*
intuition, namely one that implicitly contains the sense: if this
took place as a direct intuition, giving the object itself, it would
fulfil and verify the existential sense of this intending. The
prefigurative intuition of this verifying fulfilment furnishes
actualizing evidence — not indeed of the being, but of the
possible being of the content in question.

§ 26. *Actuality as the correlate of evident verification.*

In the first place, *formally universal problems of intentional
analysis* and pertinent investigations (already very comprehensive and difficult) concerning the *phenomenological origin of
the principles and fundamental concepts of formal logic* are indicated by these brief observations. But not only that. They advise
us of the significant fact that those concepts, with their formal-
ontological universality, point to a *universal conformity to laws
of structure on the part of conscious life,* a regularity by virtue of
which alone truth and actuality have, and / are able to have,   <95>
sense for us. To be sure, that objects in the broadest sense (real
physical things, subjective processes, numbers, states of affairs,
laws, theories, and the rest) exist for me is a statement that says
nothing immediately about evidence; it says only that objects
are accepted by me — are, in other words, there for me as cogitata intended in the positional mode: certain believing. But we
do know also that we should have to abandon such acceptance
forthwith, if a course of evident identifying synthesis were to

lead to conflict with an evident datum, and that we can be sure something is *actual* only by virtue of a synthesis of evident verification, which presents rightful or true actuality itself. It is clear that truth or the true actuality of objects is to be obtained only from *evidence*, and that it is evidence alone by virtue of which an *"actually" existing*, true, rightly accepted object of whatever form or kind *has sense for us* — and with all the determinations that for us belong to it under the title of its true nature. Every rightness comes from evidence, therefore [1] from our transcendental subjectivity itself; every imaginable adequation originates as our verification, is our synthesis, has in us its ultimate transcendental basis.

§ 27. *Habitual and potential evidence as functioning constitutively for the sense "existing object".*

To be sure, like the identity of any meant object as meant, neither the identity of the truly existing object nor the identity constituted in the adequation of the meant as such and the truly existent is a really intrinsic moment of the transient conscious process of evidence and verification. But we have here an *ideal immanence*, which refers us to further complexes of possible syntheses, as complexes that play an essential role in this connexion. Every evidence "sets up" or "institutes" for me an *abiding possession*. I can "always return" to the itself-beheld actuality, in a series of new evidences as restitutions of the first evidence. Thus, in the case of evidence of immanent data, I can return to them in a series of intuitive recollections that has the open endlessness which the "I can always do so again" (as a ‹96› horizon of potentiality) [2] creates. / Without such "possibilities" there would be for us no *fixed and abiding* being, no real and no ideal world. Both of these exist for us thanks to evidence or the presumption of being able to make evident and to repeat acquired evidence.

Hence it follows without more ado that the *particular evidence*

---

[1] Supplied in accordance with Typescript C and the French translation.

[2] Reading, with Typescript C, *"als potentieller Horizont"* instead of *"als potentiellen Horizont"*. According to the published text, the sense would be: "... the open endlessness which creates, as a horizon of potentiality, the "I can always do so again"."

does not as yet produce for us any abiding being. Everything that
exists is "in itself", in a maximally broad sense, and stands in
contrast to the accidental being "for me" of the particular acts;
likewise every truth is, in this broadest sense, a "truth in itself".
This broadest sense of the In-Itself refers us to evidence, not
however to a particular evidence as a de facto experience, but
rather to certain potentialities, which are grounded in the
transcendental Ego and his life: first of all, to the potentiality
of the [1] infinity of intendings of every kind that relate to something as identical, but then also to the potentiality of verifying
these intendings, consequently to potential evidences which, as
de facto experiences, are repeatable *in infinitum.*

§ 28. *Presumptive evidence of world-experience.*
World as an idea
correlative to a perfect experiential evidence.

In yet another and a much more complicated manner evidences refer us to infinities of evidences relating to the same
object, wherever they make their object itself-given with an
essentially necessary *one-sidedness.* That is the case with nothing
less than the totality of evidences by virtue of which a real
Objective world, as a whole and in respect of any particular
Objects, is immediately there for us intuitionally. The evidence
pertaining to particular Objects in a real Objective world is
"*external* experience"; and we can see that, as a matter of
essential necessity, no other mode of self-presentation is conceivable in the case of such objects. But we can also see that, on
the other hand, this kind of evidence has an essential "one-
sidedness" — stated more precisely: a multiform horizon of
unfulfilled anticipations (which, however, are in need of fulfilment) and, accordingly, contents of a mere meaning, which
refer us to corresponding potential evidences. This imperfect
evidence becomes more nearly perfect in the actualizing synthetic transitions from evidence to evidence, but necessarily in
such a manner that no imaginable synthesis of this kind is

[1] Reading, with Typescript C, "*diejenige der*" instead of "*die*" (the published text
as amended) or "*diejenige*" (the original typescript as given in the appendix the
published text).

completed as an adequate evidence: any such synthesis must always involve unfulfilled, expectant and accompanying
‹97› meanings. / At the same time there always remains the open possibility that the belief in being, which extends into the anticipation, will not be fulfilled, that what is appearing in the mode "it itself" nevertheless does not exist or is different. Yet, as a matter of essential necessity, external experience alone can verify objects of external experience [1], though, to be sure, it does so only as long as the (passively or actively) continuing experience has the form of a *harmonious* synthesis. That the being of the world "transcends" consciousness in this fashion (even with respect to the evidence in which the world presents itself), and that it necessarily remains transcendent, in no wise alters the fact that it is conscious life alone, wherein everything transcendent becomes constituted, as something inseparable from consciousness, and which specifically, as world-consciousness, bears within itself inseparably the sense: world — and indeed: "this actually existing" world.

Only an uncovering of the horizon of experience ultimately clarifies the "actuality" and the "transcendency" of the world, at the same time showing the world to be inseparable from transcendental subjectivity, which constitutes actuality of being and sense. The reference to harmonious infinities of further possible experience, starting from each world-experience — where "actually existing Object" can have sense only as a unity meant and meanable in the nexus of consciousness, a unity that would be given as itself in a perfect experiential evidence — manifestly signifies that an *actual* Object belonging to a world or, all the more so, *a world itself, is an infinite idea, related to infinities of harmoniously combinable experiences — an idea that is the correlate of the idea of a perfect experiential evidence*, a complete synthesis of possible experiences.

§ 29. *Material and formal ontological regions as indexes pointing to transcendental systems of evidence.*

We now understand the great tasks of the ego's self-explication, or his explication of his conscious life, which arise con-

---

[1] The phrase, "objects of external experience", supplied in accordance with Typescript C and the French translation.

cerning objectivities posited or positable in that life. The heading,
true being and truth (in all modalities), indicates, in the case of
any objects meant or ever meanable for me as transcendental
ego, a *structural differentiation among the infinite multiplicities*
of actual and possible *cogitationes* / that relate to the object in <98>
question and thus can somehow go together to make up the
unity of an identifying synthesis. *Actually existing* object indicates a *particular system* within this multiplicity, the system of
evidences relating to the object and belonging together in such
a manner that they combine to make up one (though perhaps
an infinite) *total evidence*. This would be an absolutely perfect
evidence, which would finally present the object itself in respect
of all it is — an evidence in whose synthesis everything that is
still unfulfilled expectant intention, in the particular evidences
founding the synthesis, would attain adequate fulfilment. Not
actually to produce this evidence — that would be a nonsensical
aim in the case of any Objectively real object, since (as already
observed) an absolute evidence is, in the case of such objects, an
idea — but to clear up its essential structure, or *to clear up, in
respect of all internal structures*, the essential structure of the
dimensions of infinity that make up systematically the ideal
infinite synthesis of this evidence, is a quite definite and tremendous task. It is the *problem of the transcendental constitution
of existing objectivity* (in a pregnant sense of the word <consti-
tution>). Besides formally universal investigations — that is to
say, investigations that confine themselves to the formal-logical
(formal-ontological) concept of any object as such (and thus
are indifferent to the peculiarities of the various particular categories of objects) — we have then what prove to be the tremendous problems of that constitution which occurs with respect
to each of the highest and no longer formal-logical categories
(the "regions") of objects, such as the regions subsumed under
the heading: Objective world. There is need of a *constitutional
theory* of physical Nature (which is "given" as always existing
and, in being so given, is likewise always presupposed), a constitutional theory of man, of human community, of culture, and
so forth. Each title of this kind points to a vast discipline with
different lines of investigation, corresponding to the naïve ontological component concepts (such as real space, real time, real

causality, real physical thing, real property, and so forth). Naturally it is everywhere a matter of uncovering the intentionality implicit in the experience itself as a transcendental process, a matter of explicating systematically the predelineative horizons by a conversion into possible fulfilling evidence, and then incessantly / explicating in like manner the new horizons that indeed incessantly arise within the old, according to a definite style. These explications, moreover, involve continual study of intentional correlations. As we pursue this course, an extremely complicated intentional composition of the constituting evidences, in their synthetic unity, becomes apparent as regards Objects — for example: a founding by levels of non-Objective ("merely subjective") objects, ascending from the lowest objective basis. To be this lowest basis is the continual function of immanent temporality, the flowing life that constitutes itself in and for itself. Its constitutional clarification is undertaken by the theory of original time-consciousness, wherein temporal data are constituted.[1]

⟨99⟩

---

[1] A page of stenographic text was inserted at this point in the typescript on which the published text is based. Strasser's transliteration may be rendered as follows. Time-constitution, immanency and transcendency. Single subjectivity — intersubjectivity. 1. Single subjectivity: primordial immanency, the primordial stream of consciousness, primordial facultative modification of the stream of consciousness — the course of actual experience with its de facto "I move" and with the facultative possibilities of the Ego's moving — primordial, with the sense of an abstraction from acceptances of being that involve empathy. 2. The empathies lie within the immannency that belongs to me as "ego" of the reduction. These non-originary presentations function together with all the others in the constitution of the "world". Therefore what is set forth in Meditations I-III must have made implicit use also of empathy — only it was not mentioned. The difference between other persons and me as a person among persons is itself a constituted difference — constituted within the ego. Within the ego: the transcendental differentiation between transcendental I (ego in the second sense) and transcendental others; and the transcendental intersubjective constitution of the world, as a world for all and a world that contains the transcendental subjects, mundanized as men. In the absolute and original ego of the reduction the world is constituted, as a world that is constituted as transcendentally intersubjective in every transcendental Ego. My full primordial immanency (empathy included), my concrete primordial being, constitutes as unities of being: "repetitions", "other" Egos, other total primordialities. (It already includes an abiding acceptance of them; meanwhile constitutive acceptances are continually being added.) And these transcendental others, as constituted in me, are fundamental to further constitutive functions. Their acceptedness by me, their showing themselves to me, subject to correction, is in continual synthetic connexus with everything else constituted, or in the course of being constituted, in me — but the nexus is such that the intentional repetition as others repeats this functioning too.

⟨239⟩

FOURTH MEDITATION

DEVELOPMENT OF THE CONSTITUTIONAL PROBLEMS PERTAINING TO THE TRANSCENDENTAL EGO HIMSELF

§ 30. *The transcendental ego inseparable from the processes making up his life.*

Objects exist for me, and are for me what they are, only as objects of actual and possible consciousness. If this is not to be an empty statement and a theme for empty speculations, it must be shown what makes up concretely this existence and being-thus for me, or what sort of actual and possible consciousness is concerned, what the structure of this consciousness is, what "possibility" signifies here, and so forth. This can be done solely by constitutional investigation — first, in the broader sense introduced initially, and then in the narrower sense just now described. Moreover there is but one possible method, the one demanded by the essence of intentionality and of its horizons. Even from the preparatory analyses leading us upward to the sense of the problem, it becomes clear that the transcendental ego (in the psychological parallel, the psyche) is what it is solely in relation to intentional objectivities.[1] Among these, however, are necessarily included for the ego existing objects and, for him as related to a world, not only objects within his (adequately verifiable)[2] sphere of immanent time but also world Objects, which are shown to be existent only in his inadequate, merely presumptive, external experience — in the harmoniousness of its course. / It is thus an essential property of the ego, constantly ‹100› to have systems of intentionality — among them, harmonious ones — partly as going on within him ‹actually›, partly as fixed potentialities, which, thanks to predelineating horizons, are available for uncovering. Each object that the ego ever means, thinks of, values, deals with, likewise each that he ever phantasies or can phantasy, indicates its correlative system and exists only as itself the correlate of its system.

---

[1] This sentence marked as unsatisfactory.
[2] This phrase marked as unsatisfactory.

§ 31. *The Ego as identical pole of the subjective processes.*

Now, however, we must call attention to a great gap in our exposition.[1] The ego is himself *existent for himself* in continuous evidence; thus, in himself, he is *continuously constituting himself as existing*.[2] Heretofore we have touched on only one side of this self-constitution, we have looked at only the *flowing cogito*. The ego grasps himself not only as a flowing life but also as *I*, who live this and that subjective process, who live through this and that cogito, *as the same I*. Since we were busied up to now with the intentional relation of consciousness to object, cogito to cogitatum, only that synthesis stood out for us which "polarizes" the multiplicities of actual and possible consciousness toward identical objects, accordingly in relation to *objects as poles*, synthetic unities. Now we encounter a second polarization,[3] a *second kind of synthesis*, which embraces all the particular multiplicities of *cogitationes* collectively and in its own manner, namely as belonging to the identical Ego, who, *as the active and affected subject of consciousness*, lives in all processes of consciousness and is related, *through* them, to all object-poles.

§ 32. *The Ego as substrate of habitualities.*

But it is to be noted that *this centering Ego is not an empty pole of identity*, any more than any *object* is such. Rather, according to a law of "transcendental generation", with every *act* emanating from him and having a *new* objective sense, he acquires *a new abiding property*. For example: If, in an act of judgment, I decide for the first time in favor of a being and a being-thus, the fleeting act passes; but from now on *I am*
‹101› *abidingly the Ego who is thus and so decided,* / "I am of this conviction". That, however, does not signify merely that I remember the act or can remember it later. This I can do, even if meanwhile I have "given up" my conviction. After cancellation it is no longer my conviction; but it has remained abidingly my conviction up to then. As long as it is accepted by me, I can "return"

---

[1] Author's later note: Does this not come too late?
[2] Marginal note: Transcendental Self-Constitution.
[3] Marginal note: itself a form (?) of unity-production.

to it repeatedly, and repeatedly find it as mine, habitually my
own opinion or, correlatively, find myself as the Ego who *is*
convinced, who, as the persisting Ego, is determined by this
abiding *habitus* or state. Likewise in the case of decisions of
every other kind, value-decisions, volitional decisions. I decide;
the act-process vanishes but the decision persists; whether I
become passive and sink into heavy sleep or live in other acts,
the decision continues to be accepted and, correlatively, I am
so decided from then on, as long as I do not give the decision up.
If it aims at a terminating deed, it is not "revoked" by the deed
that fulfils it; in the mode characteristic of fulfilled decision it
continues to be accepted: "I continue to stand by my deed".
I myself, who am persisting in my abiding volition, *becomed
changed* if I "cancel" my decisions or repudiate my deeds. The
persisting, the temporal enduring, of such determining properties
of the Ego, or the peculiar change that the Ego undergoes in
respect of them, manifestly is not a continuous filling of
immanent time with subjective processes — just as the abiding
Ego himself, as the pole of abiding Ego-properties, is not a
process or a continuity of processes, even though, with such
habitual determining properties, he is indeed related back to
the stream of subjective processes. Since, by his *own active gener-
ating*, the Ego constitues himself as *identical substrate of Ego-
properties*, he constitutes himself also as a "fixed and abiding"
personal Ego — in a maximally broad sense, which permits us
to speak of sub-human "persons". Though convictions are, in
general, only relatively abiding and have their modes of alteration (through modalization of the active positings — for example, "cancellation" or negation, undoing of their acceptance),
the Ego shows, in such alterations, an abiding style with a unity
of identity throughout all of them: a "personal character". /

§ 33. *The full concretion of the Ego as monad and the problem of* ‹102›
his self-constitution.

From the Ego as identical pole, and as substrate of habitualities, we distinguish *the ego taken in full concreteness* — in that
we take, in addition, that without which the Ego cannot after
all be concrete. (The ego, taken in full concreteness, we propose

to call by the Leibnizian name: monad.) The Ego can be concrete
only in the flowing multiformity of his intentional life, along with
the objects meant — and in some cases constituted as existent
for him — in that life. Manifestly, in the case of an object so
constituted, its abiding existence and being-thus are a correlate
of the habituality constituted in the Ego-pole himself by virtue
of his position-taking.

That is to be understood in the following manner. As ego, I
have a surrounding world, which is continually "existing for
me"; and, in it, objects as "existing for me" — already with the
abiding distinction between those with which I am acquainted
and those only anticipated as objects with which I may become
acquainted. The former, the ones that are, in the first sense,
existent for me, are such by original acquisition — that is: by
my original taking cognizance of what I had never beheld previously, and my explication of it in particular intuitions of its
features. Thereby, in my synthetic activity, the object becomes
constituted originally, perceptively, in the explicit sense-form:
"something identical having its manifold properties", or "object
as identical with itself and undergoing determination in respect
of its manifold properties". This, my activity of positing and
explicating being, sets up a habituality of my Ego, by virtue of
which the object, as having its manifold determinations, is mine
abidingly. Such abiding acquisitions make up my surrounding
world, so far as I am acquainted with it at the time, with its
horizons of objects with which I am unacquainted — that is:
objects yet to be acquired but already anticipated with this
formal object-structure.

I exist for myself and am continually given to myself,[1] by
experiential evidence, as "*I myself*". This is true of the transcendental ego and, correspondingly, of the psychologically pure
ego; it is true, moreover, with respect to any sense of the word
ego. Since the monadically concrete ego includes also the whole
of actual and potential conscious life, it is clear that the problem
of *explicating this monadic ego phenomenologically* (the problem
‹103› of his constitution for himself) must / include *all constitutional
problems without exception*. Consequently the phenomenology of
this *self-constitution* coincides with *phenomenology as a whole*.

---

[1] Reading: *Ich bin für mich selbst und* ‹*bin*› *mir ... gegeben.*

§ 34. *A fundamental development of phenomenological method.
Transcendental analysis as eidetic.*

With the doctrine of the Ego as pole of his acts and substrate
of habitualities, we have already touched on the *problems of
phenomenological genesis* and done so at a significant point. Thus
we have touched the level of *genetic phenomenology.* Before we
clarify the more precise sense of genetic phenomenology, a
renewed meditation concerning phenomenological method is needed.
At last we must bring to bear a fundamental methodological
insight, which, once it is grasped, pervades the whole phenomenological method (and likewise, in the natural realm, the method
of a genuine and pure internal psychology). We have delayed
mentioning it, only to facilitate entrance into phenomenology.
The excessively great multiplicity of novel discoveries and
problems was meant to act at first in the simpler attire of a
merely empirical description (though conducted purely within
the sphere of transcendental experience). The *method of eidetic
description,* however, signifies a transfer of all empirical descriptions into a new and fundamental dimension, which at the
beginning would have increased the difficulties of understanding;
on the other hand, it is easy to grasp after a considerable number
of empirical [1] descriptions.

By the method of transcendental reduction each of us, as
Cartesian [2] meditator, was led back to his transcendental ego —
naturally with its concrete-monadic contents as this de facto
ego, the one and only absolute ego. When I keep on meditating,
I, as this ego, find descriptively formulable, intentionally explicatable types; and I was able to progress step by step in the
intentional uncovering of my "monad" along the fundamental
lines that offer themselves. For good reasons, in the course of
our descriptions such expressions as "essential necessity" and
"essentially determined" forced themselves upon us — phrases
in which a definite concept of the Apriori, first clarified and
delimited by phenomenology, receives expression. /

What is involved here will become clear directly in particular ‹104›
examples. Let us pick out no matter what type of intentional

---

[1] Crossed out.
[2] Replaced by "transcendental".

processes (of perception, retention, recollection, declaration, liking something, striving for it, and so forth) and think of it as explicated and described in respect of its sort of intentional performance — accordingly: in respect of noesis and noema. This can signify (and so we have understood it up to now) that types of de facto occurences in the de facto transcendental ego are in question and that the transcendental descriptions are therefore meant to have an "empirical" significance. But involuntarily we confined our description to such a universality that its results remain unaffected, regardless of what the situation may be with respect to the empirical factualness of the transcendental ego.

Let us make this clear to ourselves, and then fruitful for our method. Starting from this table-perception as an example, we vary the perceptual object, table, with a completely free optionalness, yet in such a manner that we keep perception fixed as perception of something, no matter what. Perhaps we begin by fictively changing the shape or the color of the object quite arbitrarily, keeping identical only its perceptual appearing. In other words: Abstaining from acceptance of its being, we change the fact of this perception into a pure possibility, one among other quite "optional" pure possibilities — but possibilities that are possible perceptions. We, so to speak, shift the actual perception into the realm of non-actualities, the realm of the as-if, which supplies us with "pure" possibilities, pure of everything that restricts to this fact or to any fact whatever. As regards the latter point, we keep the aforesaid possibilities, not as restricted even to the co-posited de facto ego, but just as a completely free "imaginableness" of phantasy. Accordingly from the very start we might have taken as our initial example a phantasying ourselves into a perceiving, with no relation to the rest of our de facto life. Perception, the universal type thus acquired, floats in the air, so to speak — in the atmosphere of pure phantasiableness [1]. Thus removed from all factualness, it has become the pure "*eidos*" perception, whose "*ideal*" extension is made up of all ideally possible perceptions, as purely phantsiable processes. <105> / Analyses of perception are then "*essential*" or "*eidetic*" analyses. All that we have set forth concerning syntheses belonging to the

[1] Reading, with Typescript C, the singular.

type, perception, concerning horizons of potentiality, and so forth, holds good, as can easily be seen, *"essentially"* for everything formable in this free variation, accordingly for all imaginable perceptions without exception — in other words: with absolute *"essential universality"*, and with *"essential necessity"* for every particular case selected, hence for every de facto perception, since every *fact can be thought of merely as exemplifying a pure possibility.*

The variation being meant as an evident one, accordingly as presenting in pure intuition the possibilites themselves as possibilities, its correlate is an *intuitive and apodictic consciousness of something universal.* The eidos itself is a beheld or beholdable universal, one that is pure, "unconditioned" — that is to say: according to its own intuitional sense, a universal not conditioned by any fact. It is *prior to all "concepts"*, in the sense of verbal significations; indeed, as pure concepts, these must be made to fit the eidos.

Though each singly selected type is thus elevated from its milieu within the empirically factual transcendental ego into the pure eidetic sphere, the intentional outer horizons pointing to its uncoverable connexus within the ego do not vanish; only this *nexus-horizon itself becomes eidetic.* In other words: With each eidetically pure type we find ourselves, not indeed inside the de facto ego, but *inside an eidos ego*; and constitution of one actually pure possibility among others carries with it implicitly, as its outer horizon, a *purely possible ego*, a pure possibility-variant of my *de facto* ego. We could have started out by imagining this ego to be freely varied, and could set the problem of exploring eidetically the explicit constitution of any transcendental ego whatever. The new phenomenology did so from the beginning; and accordingly all the descriptions and all the problem-delimitations treated by us up to now have in fact been translations from the original eidetic form back into that of an empirical description of types. Therefore, if we think of *a phenomenology* developed as an intuitively apriori science *purely according to the eidetic method,* all its eidetic researches are nothing else but *uncoverings of the | all-embracing eidos, transcendental* ‹106› *ego as such*, which comprises all pure possibility-variants of my de facto ego and this ego itself qua possibility. Eidetic phenomenology, accordingly, explores the universal Apriori without which neither I nor [1] any transcendental Ego whatever is "imaginable"; or, since every eidetic universality has the value of an unbreakable law, eidetic phenomenology explores the all-embracing laws that prescribe for every factual statement about something transcendental the possible sense (as opposed to the absurdity or inconsistency) of that statement.

[2] To me as the meditating ego [3], guided by the idea of a philosophy as the all-embracing science, grounded with absolute strictness, a science whose possibility I took as a tentative basis, it becomes evident after these last considerations that, *first of all*, I must develop a purely *eidetic phenomenology* and that in the latter alone the first actualization of a philosophical science — the actualization of a "first philosophy" — takes place or can take place. After transcendental reduction, my true interest is directed to my pure ego, to the uncovering of this de facto ego. But the uncovering can become genuinely scientific, only if I go back to the apodictic principles that pertain to this ego as exemplifying the eidos ego: the essential universalities and necessities by means of which the fact is to be related to its rational grounds (those of its pure possibility) and thus made scientific (logical). It should be noted that, in the transition from my ego to an ego as such, neither the actuality nor the possibility of other egos is presupposed. I phantasy only myself as if I were otherwise; I do not phantasy others. "In itself", then, the science of pure possibilites precedes the science of actualities and alone makes it possible, as a science. With this we attain the methodological insight that, *along with phenomenological reduction, eidetic intuition is the fundamental form of all particular transcendental methods* (that both of them determine, through and through, the legitimate sense of a transcendental phenomenology). /

<107>   § 35. *Excursus into eidetic internal psychology.*

We go outside the closed sphere of our meditations, which restricts us to transcendental phenomenology, if we cannot

---

[1] Inserted (substituted?) here: any possibility-variant.
[2] A new section indicated marginally.
[3] Originally: the ego meditating in a Cartesian fashion.

repress the remark that, with only slight modifications (which, to be sure, abolish its transcendental sense), the whole content of the fundamental methodological observation that has just been made remains ours when, on the basis of the natural world view, we strive for a psychology as a positive science and, in that connexion, strive primarily for the psychology that is first in itself and necessary to any psychology: purely intentional psychology. To the concrete transcendental ego there corresponds then the human Ego, concretely as the psyche taken purely in itself and ‹as it is › for itself, with the psychic polarization: I as pole of my habitualities, the properties comprised in my character. Instead of eidetic transcendental phenomenology we then have an eidetic pure psychology, relating to the eidos psyche, whose eidetic horizon, to be sure, remains unexamined. If, however, it did become examined, the way to overcome this positivity would become open — that is, the way leading over into absolute phenomenology, the phenomenology of the transcendental ego, who indeed no longer has a horizon that could lead beyond the sphere of his transcendental being and thus relativize him.

§ 36. *The transcendental ego as the universe of possible forms of subjective process. The compossibility of subjective processes in coexistence or succession as subject to eidetic laws.*

After the significant new formulation of the idea of a transcendental phenomenology according to the eidetic method, when we return to the task of discovering the problems of phenomenology, we naturally confine ourselves thenceforth within the limits of a purely eidetic phenomenology, in which the de facto transcendental ego and particular data given in transcendental experience of the ego have the significance merely of examples of pure possibilities. Likewise we understand the already discovered problems as eidetic, in that we think of the possibility of making them eidetically pure (a possibility shown in our example) as actualized. / Satisfying the ideal problem of an actually systematic ‹108› discovery of the essential components belonging to a concrete ego as such, or initiating an actually *systematic sequence of problems and investigations*, involves extraordinary difficulties.

Only in the last decade has this system begun to make itself clear, above all because we have gained [1] new ways of access to the *specifically universal* problems of the transcendental ego's constitution. The universal Apriori pertaining to a transcendental ego as such is an eidetic form, which contains an infinity of forms, an infinity of apriori types of actualities and potentialities of life, along with the objects constitutable in a life as objects actually existing. But in a *unitarily possible* ego [2] not all singly possible types are *compossible*, and not all compossible ones are compossible in just any order, at no matter what loci in that ego's own temporality. If I form some scientific theory or other, my complex rational activity, with its rationally constituted existent, belongs to an essential type that is possible, not in every possible ego,[3] but only in one that is "rational" in a particular sense, the same that, with the mundanization of the ego, presents itself in the essential form: man [4] ("rational" animal). When I reduce my de facto theorizing to its eidetic type, I have varied myself too (regardless of whether I am aware of it) — not however in a wholly optional manner, but within the frame of the corresponding essential type, "rational" being. Manifestly I cannot imagine the theorizing I do or can do now as shifted arbitrarily within the unity of my life; and this too carries over into the eidetic. Eidetic apprehension of my (transcendentally reduced) childhood life and its possibilities of constitution produces a type, such that in its further development, but not in its own nexus, the type "scientific theorizing" can occur. Restriction of this kind has its grounds in an apriori universal structure, in a conformity to universal eidetic laws of coexistence and succession in egological time. For indeed whatever occurs in my ego,[5] and eidetically in an ego as such — in the way of intentional processes, constituted unities, Ego habitualities — has its temporality and, in this respect, participates in the system of forms that belongs to the all-inclusive temporality

---

[1] Typescript C and the French translation. The published text: "difficulties, above all because we must gain".

[2] Later: in any unitarily possible ego that is a possibility-variant of my de facto ego.

[3] Later: not in every possibility-variant of my ego.

[4] Later: I, the man.

[5] Later: occurs as related to me.

with which every imaginable ego, every possibility-variant of
my ego,[1] constitutes himself for himself. /

§ 37. *Time as the universal form of all egological genesis.*   <109>

The eidetic laws of compossibility (rules that govern simultaneous or successive existence and possible existence together,
in the fact) are laws of causality in a maximally broad sense —
laws for an If and Then. Yet it is better to avoid here the expression causality, which is laden with prejudices (deriving
from naturalism) [2], and to speak of *motivation* in the transcendental sphere (and in the sphere of "pure" psychology). The
universe of subjective processes, which are the "really inherent"
consciousness-constituents of the transcendental ego, is a universe of compossibilities only in the universal *unity-form of the
flux*, in which all particulars have their respective places as
processes that flow within it. Accordingly even this most universal form, which belongs to all particular forms of concrete
subjective processes (with the products that are flowingly constituted in the flux of such processes) is the form of a motivation,
connecting all and governing within each single process in particular. We can call it furthermore a *formal regularity pertaining
to a universal genesis*, which is such that past, present, and
future, become unitarily constituted over and over again, in a
certain noetic-noematic formal structure of flowing modes of
givenness.

But, within this form, life goes on as a motivated course of
particular constitutive performances with a multiplicity of
particular motivations and motivational systems, which, according to *universal laws of genesis*, produce a unity of *universal
genesis of the ego*. The ego constitutes himself for himself in, so
to speak, the unity of a "history". We said that the constitution
of the ego contains all the constitutions of all the objectivities
existing for him, whether these be immanent or transcendent,
ideal or real. It should now be added that the *constitutive systems*
(systems actualizable by the Ego) [3], by virtue of which such and

---

[1] This phrase inserted later.
[2] Added later.
[3] Inserted later.

such objects and categories of objects exist [1] for him, are themselves possible only within the frame of a genesis in conformity with laws. At the same time they are bound, in their constituting, by the universal genetic form that makes the concrete ego (the monad) possible as a unity, as having particular constituents of his being that are compossible. That a Nature, a cultural world, a world of men with their social forms, and so forth, exist for me signifies that possibilities of corresponding experiences exist for me, as experiences I can at any <110> time / bring into play and continue in a certain *synthetic style*, whether or not I am at present actually experiencing objects belonging to the realm in question. It signifies furthermore that other modes of consciousness corresponding to them — vague intendings and the like — exist as possibilities for me, and also that these other modes of consciousness have possibilities of becoming fulfilled or disappointed by experiences of predelineated types. This involves a firmly developed habituality, acquired by a certain genesis in conformity with eidetic laws.

We are reminded here of the long-familiar problems concerning the *psychological origin* of the "idea of space", the "idea of time", the "idea of a physical thing", and so forth. In phenomenology such problems present themselves as transcendental and, naturally, as *problems of intentionality*, which have their particular places among the problems of a universal genesis.

Access to the ultimate universalities involved in problems of eidetic phenomenology is, however, very difficult. This is particularly true with respect to an *ultimate genesis*. The beginning phenomenologist is bound involuntarily by the circumstance that he takes himself as his initial example. Transcendentally he finds himself as the ego, then as generically an ego, who already has (in conscious fashion) a world — a world of our universally familiar ontological type, with Nature, with culture (sciences, fine art, mechanical art, and so forth), with personalities of a higher order (state, church), and the rest. The phenomenology developed at first is merely "static"; its descriptions are analogous to those of natural history, which concern particular types and, at best, arrange them in their systematic order. Questions of universal genesis and the genetic structure

---

[1] Changed to: are accepted unities.

of the ego in his universality, so far as that structure is more than temporal [1] formation, are still far away; and, indeed, they belong to a higher level. [2] But even when they are raised, it is with a restriction. At first, even eidetic observation will consider an ego as such with the restriction that a constituted world already exists for him. This, moreover, is a necessary level; only by laying open the law-forms of the genesis pertaining to this level can one see the possibilities of a *maximally universal* eidetic phenomenology. In the latter the ego varies himself so freely that he does not keep even the ideal restrictive presupposition that a world / having the ontological structure accepted by us ‹111› as obvious is essentially constituted for him.

§ 38. *Active and passive genesis.*

If we inquire first about principles of constitutive genesis that have universal significance for us, as possible subjects related to a world, we find them to be divided according to two fundamental forms, into principles of *active* and principles of *passive* genesis. In active genesis the Ego functions as productively constitutive, by means of subjective processes that are specifically acts of the Ego. Here belong all the works of *practical reason*, in a maximally broad sense. In this sense even logical reason is practical. The characteristic feature (in the case of the realm of logos) [3] is that Ego-acts, pooled in a sociality — whose transcendental sense, to be sure, we have not yet brought to light —, become combined in a manifold, specifically active synthesis and, on the basis of objects already given (in modes of consciousness that give beforehand), *constitute new objects originally.* These then present themselves for consciousness *as products.* Thus, in collecting, the collection ‹is constituted ›; in counting, the number; in dividing, the part; in predicating, the predicate and the predicational complex of affairs; in inferring, the inference; and so forth. Original universality-consciousness is likewise an activity, one in which the universal becomes constituted objectively. On the Ego side there becomes constituted a conse-

---

[1] Marginal note: immanent?
[2] The rest of this paragraph is marked as unsatisfactory.
[3] Inserted later.

quent habituality of continuing acceptance, which thereupon is part of the constitution of the object as simply existing for the Ego: an object that can always be seized again, be it in reiterated producings, with synthetic consciousness of the same objectivity as given again in *"categorial intuition"*, or be it in a synthetically appertinent vague consciousness. The transcendental constitution of such objects (cultural objects, for example), in relation to *intersubjective* activities, presupposes the antecedent constitution of a transcendental intersubjectivity — about which we shall not speak until later.[1] /

<112> As already mentioned, the higher forms of such activities of "reason" in a specific sense and, correlatively, the higher forms of *products* of reason, all of which have the character of *irreality* (that of "ideal" objects), cannot be regarded forthwith as belonging to every concrete ego as such. This is already shown by memory of our childhood. However, as regards the *lowest levels*, such as experiential grasping, explicating the experienced[2] in respect of its parts, taking together, relating, and the like, the situation may well turn out to be different. In any case, anything built by activity necessarily presupposes, as the lowest level, a passivity that gives something beforehand; and, when we trace anything built actively, we run into constitution by passive generation. The "ready-made" object that confronts us in life as an existent mere physical thing (when we disregard all the "spiritual" or "cultural" characteristics that make it knowable as, for example, a hammer, a table, an aesthetic creation) is given, with the originality of the "it itself", in the synthesis of a passive experience. As such a thing, it is given beforehand to "spiritual" activities, which begin with active grasping.

While these are making their synthetic products, the passive synthesis that supplies all their "material" still goes on. The physical thing given beforehand in passive intuition continues to appear in a unitary intuition; and, no matter how much the thing may be modified therein by the activity of explication, of grasping parts and features, it continues to be given beforehand

---

[1] This sentence marked as unsatisfactory.

[2] Reading *"das Erfahrene"* instead of *"das Erfahren"* (experiencing), as in both the published text and Typescript C.

during and in this activity: The manifold modes of appearance, the unitary visual or tactual "perceptual images" continue their flow; and, in their manifestly passive synthesis, the one physical thing, with its one shape and other unitary features, appears. Yet precisely this synthesis, as a synthesis having this form, has its "history", evinced in the synthesis itself. It is owing to an essentially necessary genesis that I, the ego, can experience a physical thing and do so even at first glance. This is true, moreover, not only as regards phenomenological genesis but also as regards genesis in the usual sense, psychological genesis. With good reason it is said that in infancy we had to learn to see physical things, and that such modes of consciousness of them had to precede all others genetically. In "early infancy", then, the field of perception that gives beforehand does not as yet contain anything that, in a mere look, might be explicated as a physical thing. Yet, without putting ourselves back into the realm of passivity, to say nothing of using the external psychophysical point of view of psychology, / we can, the meditating ‹113› ego can, penetrate into the intentional constituents of experiential phenomena themselves — thing-experiencing phenomena and all others — and thus find intentional references leading back to a "history" and accordingly making these phenomena knowable as formations subsequent to other, essentially antecedent formations (even if the latter cannot be related to precisely the same constituted object). There, however, we soon encounter eidetic laws governing a passive forming of perpetually new syntheses (a forming that, in part, lies prior to all activity and, in part, takes in all activity itself); we encounter a passive genesis of the manifold apperceptions, as products that persist in a habituality relating specifically to them. When these habitual apperceptions become actually operative, the already given objects formed for the central Ego appear[1], affect him, and motivate activities. Thanks to the aforesaid passive synthesis (into which the performances of active synthesis also enter), the Ego always has an environment of "objects". Even the circumstance that everything affecting me, as a "developed" ego, is apperceived as an "object", a substrate of predicates with which I may become acquainted, belongs here, since this is an

[1] Crossed out.

already familiar goal-form for possible explications as acquaintive explications — explications that would constitute an object as an abiding possession, as something accessible again and again; and this goal-form is understandable in advance as having arisen from a genesis. It itself points back to a "primal instituting" of this form. Everything known to us points to an original becoming acquainted; what we call unknown has, nevertheless, a known structural form: the form "object" and, more particularly, the form "spatial thing", "cultural Object", "tool", and so forth.

§ 39. *Association as a principle of passive genesis.*

The *universal principle of passive genesis*, for the constitution of all objectivities given completely prior to the products of activity [1], bears the title *association*. Association, it should be clearly noted, is a matter of *intentionality*, descriptively demonstrable as that, in respect of its primal forms, and standing, in respect of its intentional performances, under *eidetic laws*. Owing to these, each and every passive constitution is to be made understandable — both the constitution of subjective processes, as objects in immanent time, and the constitution of all real natural objects belonging to the Objective spatio-tempo-
‹114› ral world. Association is a / *fundamental concept belonging to transcendental phenomenology* (and, in the psychological parallel, a fundamental concept belonging to a purely intentional psychology). The old concepts of association and of laws of association, though they too have usually been related to the coherencies of pure psychic life by Hume and later thinkers, are only naturalistic distortions of the corresponding genuine, intentional concepts. From phenomenology, which was very late in finding avenues to the exploration of association, this concept receives a completely new aspect, an essentially new delimitation, with new fundamental forms. Here belongs, for example, sensuous configuration in coexistence and in succession. It is phenomenologically evident, but strange to the tradition-bound, that

---

[1] Reading (somewhat freely) with the published text, *"den aktiven Gebilden letztlich vorgegebenen"*, instead of with the same as amended, *"im aktiven Gebilden letztlich vorgegebenen"*.

association is not a title merely for a conformity to empirical laws on the part of complexes of data comprised in a "psyche" — according to the old figure, something like an intrapsychic gravitation — but a title (moreover an extremely comprehensive one) for a conformity to eidetic laws on the part of the constitution of the pure ego. It designates a *realm of the "innate" Apriori*, without which an ego as such is unthinkable. Only through the phenomenology of genesis does the ego become understandable: as a nexus, connected in the unity of an all-embracing genesis, an infinite nexus of synthetically congruous performances — at levels, all of which fit the universal persisting form, *temporality*, because the latter itself is built up in a continual, passive and completely universal genesis, which, as a matter of essential necessity, embraces everything new. In the developed ego, this many-leveled structure is conserved as a persistent form-system of apperception and consequently of constituted objectivities — among them, the ones belonging to an Objective universe having a fixed ontological structure; and this conserving is itself only a form of genesis. In all of that, the particular fact is irrational; but it is possible only in the apriori form-system pertaining to it as an egological fact. Nor should it be overlooked here that *"fact"*, with its *"irrationality"*, is itself a *structural concept within the system of the concrete Apriori*.

§ 40. *Transition to the question of transcendental idealism.*

Now that the problems of phenomenology have been reduced to the unitary comprehensive title, "the (static and genetic) constitution of objectivities of possible consciousness", / phe- ‹115› nomenology seems to be rightly characterized also as *transcendental theory of knowledge*. Let us contrast theory of knowledge, as transcendental in our sense, with traditional theory of knowledge.

The latter's problem is transcendence. Even when the traditional theory, as empiristic, bases itself on the usual psychology, it intends, not to be merely psychology of knowledge, but to clear up the essential possibility of knowledge. The problem arises for it, and is dealt with, in the natural attitude. I find myself here as a man in the world; likewise as experiencing and scientifically knowing the world, myself included. And now I say to myself: Whatever exists for me, exists for me thanks to my knowing consciousness; it is for me the experienced of my experiencing, the thought of my thinking, the theorized of my theorizing, the intellectually seen of my insight. If, following Brentano,[1] I recognize intentionality, I shall say: Intentionality, as a fundamental property of my psychic life, is a real [2] property belonging to me, as a man, and to every other man in respect of his purely psychic inner being. (Indeed, Brentano had already made intentionality central for empirical human psychology.) [3] The first person singular of this beginning is, and remains, the natural first person singular; it confines itself, and likewise the whole further treatment of the problem, within the realm of the given world. Accordingly I go on to say, and quite understandably: Whatever exists for a man like me and is accepted by him, exists for him and is accepted in his own conscious life, which, in all consciousness of a world and in all scientific doing, keeps to itself. All my distinguishing between genuine and deceptive experience and between being and illusion in experience goes on within the sphere itself of my consciousness; the like is true when I distinguish, at a higher level, between thinking with and without insight, or between what is necessary a priori and what is inconsistent, or, again, between the empirically correct and the empirically false. Evidently actual, intellectually necessary, inconsistent, thinkable, probable, and the like — all these are characteristics that occur within the realm itself of my consciousness, as characteristics of the intentional object in question. Every grounding, every showing of truth and being, goes on wholly within myself; and its result is a characteristic in the cogitatum of my cogito. /

‹116›   Therein lies the great problem, according to the traditional view. That I attain certainties, even compelling evidences, in my own domain of consciousness, in the nexus of motivation determining me, is understandable. But how can this business, going on wholly within the immanency of conscious life, acquire Objective significance? How can evidence (*clara et distincta*

---

[1] This phrase crossed out.
[2] Crossed out. Exclamation point in the margin.
[3] The original of these last two sentences marked as unsatisfactory

perceptio) claim to be more than a characteristic of consciousness within me? Aside from the (perhaps not so unimportant) exclusion of acceptance of the world as being, it is the Cartesian problem, which was supposed to be solved by divine *veracitas*.

§ 41. *Genuine phenomenological explication of one's own "ego cogito" as transcendental idealism.*

What does phenomenology's transcendental self-investigation have to say about this? Nothing less than that the whole problem is inconsistent. It involves an inconsistency into which Descartes necessarily fell, because he missed the genuine sense of his reduction to the indubitable — we were about to say: his transcendental epoché and reduction to the pure ego. But, precisely because of its complete disregard of the Cartesian epoché, the usual post-Cartesian way of thinking is much cruder. We ask: Who then is the Ego who can rightly ask such "transcendental" questions? As a natural man, can I rightly ask them? As a natural man, can I ask seriously and transcendentally how I get outside my island of consciousness and how what presents itself in my consciousness as a subjective evidence-process can acquire Objective significance? When I apperceive myself as a natural man, I have already apperceived the spatial world and construed myself as in space, where I already have an Outside Me. Therefore the validity of world-apperception has already been presupposed, has already entered into the sense assumed in asking the question — whereas the answer alone ought to show the rightness of accepting anything as Objectively valid. Manifestly the conscious execution of phenomenological reduction is needed, in order to attain that Ego and conscious life by which transcendental questions, as questions about the possibility of transcendent knowledge, can be asked. But as soon as — instead of transiently exercising a phenomenological epoché — one sets to work, attempting in a systematic self-investigation and as the pure ego to uncover this ego's whole field of consciousness, one recognizes that all that / exists for the pure ego becomes consti- ⟨117⟩ tuted in him himself; furthermore, that every kind of being — including every kind characterized as, in any sense, "transcendent" — has its own particular constitution. Transcendency

in every form is an immanent existential characteristic, constituted within the ego. Every imaginable sense, every imaginable
being, whether the latter is called immanent or transcendent,
falls within the domain of transcendental subjectivity, as the
subjectivity that constitutes sense and being. The attempt to
conceive the universe of true being as something lying outside
the universe of possible consciousness, possible knowledge, possible evidence, the two being related to one another merely externally by a rigid law, is nonsensical. They belong together
essentially; and, as belonging together essentially, they are also
concretely one, one in the only absolute concretion: transcendental subjectivity. If transcendental subjectivity is the universe of possible sense, then an outside is precisely — nonsense.
But even nonsense is always a mode of sense and has its non-
sensicalness within the sphere of possible insight. That is true,
however, not alone in the case of the merely de facto ego and
what is in fact (thanks to his own constituting) [1] accessible to
him as existing for him — including an open plurality of other
egos who, along with their constitutive performances, exist for
him.[2] Stated more precisely: If (as is in fact the case) there are
transcendentally constituted in me, the transcendental ego, not
only other egos but also (as constituted in turn by the transcendental intersubjectivity accruing to me thanks to the constitution in me of others) an Objective world common to us all,
then everything said up to now is true, not alone in the case of
my de facto ego and in the case of this de facto intersubjectivity
and world, which receive sense and existence-status in my
subjectivity [3]. The "phenomenological self-explication" that
went on in my ego, this explication of all my ego's constitutings
and all the objectivities existing for him, necessarily assumed
the methodic form of an apriori self-explication, one that gives
the facts their place in the corresponding universe of pure (or
eidetic) possibilities. This explication therefore concerns my de
facto ego, only [4] so far as the latter is one of the pure possibilities
to be acquired by his free phantasy-variation (fictive changing)

of himself.[1] Therefore, as eidetic, the explication is valid for the universe of these, my possibilities as essentially an ego, my possibilities namely of being otherwise; accordingly then it is valid also for every possible / intersubjectivity related (with a <118> corresponding modification) to these possibilities, and valid likewise for every world imaginable as constituted in such an intersubjectivity. Genuine theory of knowledge is accordingly possible [sinnvoll] only as a transcendental-phenomenological theory, which, instead of operating with inconsistent inferences leading from a supposed immanency to a supposed transcendency (that of no matter what "thing in itself", which is alleged to be essentially unknowable), has to do exclusively with systematic clarification of the knowledge performance, a clarification in which this must become thoroughly understandable as an intentional performance [2]. Precisely thereby every sort of existent itself, real or ideal, becomes understandables as a "product" of transcendental subjectivity, a product constituted in just that performance. This kind of understandablenes is the highest imaginable form of rationality. All wrong interpretations of being come from naïve blindness to the horizons that join in determining the sense of being, and to the corresponding tasks of uncovering implicit intentionality. If these are seen and undertaken, there results a universal phenomenology, as a self-explication of the ego, carried out with continuous evidence and at the same time with concreteness. Stated more precisely: First, a self-explication in the pregnant sense, showing systematically how the ego constitutes himself, in respect of his own proper essence, as existent in himself and for himself; then, secondly, a self-explication in the broadened sense, which goes on from there to show how, by virtue of this proper essence, the ego likewise constitutes in himself something "other", something "Objective", and thus constitutes everything without exception that ever has for him, in the Ego, existential status as non-Ego.[3]

[1] The whole passage beginning approximately with "That is true, however ..." marked as unsatisfactory. A few lines beyond here, the comment: "That will have to be treated differently."

[2] The phrase rendered as "understandable as an intentional performance" marked as unsatisfactory.

[3] Exclamation point in margin opposite the last clause. Three exclamation points opposite the passage beginning with "Stated more precisely ...". The whole passage from there, presumably to the end of the paragraph, marked as unsatisfactory.

Carried out with this systematic concreteness, phenomenology is *eo ipso "transcendental idealism"*, though in a fundamentally and essentially new sense. It is not a psychological idealism, and most certainly not such an idealism as sensualistic psychologism proposes, an idealism that would derive a senseful world from senseless sensuous data. Nor is it a Kantian idealism, which believes it can keep open, at least as a limiting concept, the possibility of a world of things in themselves [1]. On the contrary, we have here a transcendental idealism that *is* nothing more than a consequentially executed self-explication in the form of a systematic egological science, an explication of my ego as subject of every possible cognition, and indeed with respect to every sense of what exists, wherewith the latter might be able to *have* a sense for me, the ego. This idealism is not a product of sportive <119> argumentations, a prize / to be won in the dialectical contest with "realisms". It is *sense-explication* achieved *by actual work*, an explication carried out as regards every type of existent ever conceivable by me, the ego, and specifically as regards the transcendency actually given to me beforehand through experience: Nature, culture, the world as a whole. But that signifies: systematic uncovering of the constituting intentionality itself. *The proof of this idealism is therefore phenomenology itself.* Only someone who misunderstands either the deepest sense of intentional method, or that of transcendental reduction, or perhaps both, can attempt to separate phenomenology from transcendental idealism. Whoever labors under the first misunderstanding has not advanced even so far as to grasp the peculiar essence of a genuine intentional psychology (including that of an intentional-psychological theory of knowledge) or the requirement that intentional psychology become the fundamental and central part of a truly scientific psychology. On the other hand, anyone who misconstrues the sense and performance of transcendental-phenomenological reduction is still entangled in psychologism; he confounds intentional psychology and transcendental phenomenology, a parallel that arises by virtue of the essential possibility of a change in attitude; he falls a victim to the incon-

---

[1] Added later: which would signify for the Ego a realm in itself, belonging to him mythically. And Kantian transcendentalism would by no means turn into the phenomenological transcendentalism treated here, even if such doctrines were eliminated.

sistency of a transcendental philosophy that stays within the natural realm.

Our meditations have prospered to the extent that already they have made evident the necessary style of a philosophy, namely its style as transcendental-phenomenological philosophy, and correlatively, for the universe of what exists for us actually or possibly, the style of its only possible sense-interpretation: the style of the latter as transcendental-phenomenological idealism. Included in this evidence is the insight that the infinity of tasks disclosed by our extremely general preliminary sketch — the self-explications of my (the meditator's) ego in respect of constituting and constituted — are a chain of particular meditations fitting into the universal frame of one unitary meditation, which can always be carried further synthetically.

Are we allowed to break off with this and leave all the rest to an exposition of particulars? Is the acquired evidence, with its predelineative goal-sense, already sufficient? Has the predelineation already been carried far enough to fill us with that great belief in a / philosophy arising from this meditative method of ‹120› self-explication —- so that we can accept such a philosophy as an aim of our life-will and go to work with happy assurance? Even in our fleeting glance at what is constituted in us — in me always, in the meditating ego — as a world, a whole universe of being, we naturally could not avoid being mindful of "others" and their constitutings. By means of the alien constitutings constituted in my own self, there becomes constituted for me (as has already been mentioned) the common world for "all of us". Here belongs also, of course, the constituting of a philosophy as common to "all of us" who meditate together — ideally, a single *philosophia perennis*. But will our evidence stand firm, the evidence of a phenomenological philosophy and a phenomenological idealism as the only possibilities — this evidence, which was completely clear and certain to us as long as we devoted ourselves to the course of our meditative intuitions and stated the essential necessities that came to light in them? Will it not become unstable, since we have not carried our methodic predelineations through to the point where the possibility of the being for me of others (as we all feel, a very puzzling possibility) and the more precise nature of their being for me are understandable and since the complex problem of their being for me has not been explicated? If our "Cartesian meditations" are to be, for us nascent philosophers, the genuine "introduction" into a philosophy and the beginning that establishes the actuality of a philosophy as a necessarily practical idea (a beginning to which belongs therefore the evidence of a course — constitutable [1] as an ideal necessity — for an infinity of executing work), then our meditations themselves must carry us so far that, in this respect, they leave no puzzles as to the course and the goal. In full accordance with the aspiration of the old Cartesian meditations, ours must have uncovered and made understandable without residue the universal problems relating to the final idea of philosophy (for us, therefore, the universal problems of constitution); and that implies that they must have already exposed with the greatest, yet with a strictly comprehended, universality the true universal sense of "the existent as such" and of its universal structures — with a universality that makes possible, for the first time, executive ontological work, in the form of a concretely connected phenomenological philosophy, and then <121> in consequence a philosophical / science of matters of fact. For philosophy, and accordingly for the correlational research of phenomenology, "the existent" is a practical idea, that of the infinity of theoretically determining work.

---

[1] Reading *"zu konstituierenden"* instead of simply *"konstituierenden"* (constituting), as in both the published text and Typescript C.

FIFTH MEDITATION

UNCOVERING OF THE SPHERE OF TRANSCENDENTAL BEING AS MONADOLOGICAL INTERSUBJECTIVITY

§ 42. *Exposition of the problem of experiencing someone else, in rejoinder to the objection that phenomenology entails solipsism.*

As the point of departure for our new meditations, let us take what may seem to be a grave objection. The objection concerns nothing less than the claim of transcendental phenomenology to be itself transcendental *philosophy* and therefore its claim that, in the form of a constitutional problematic and theory moving within the limits of the transcendentally reduced ego, it can solve the transcendental problems pertaining to the *Objective world.* When I, the meditating I, reduce myself to my absolute transcendental ego by phenomenological epoché do I not become *solus ipse*; and do I not remain that, as long as I carry on a consistent self-explication under the name phenomenology? Should not a phenomenology that proposed to solve the problems of Objective being, and to present itself actually as philosophy, be branded therefore as transcendental solipsism?

Let us consider the matter more closely. Transcendental reduction restricts me to the stream of my pure conscious processes and the unities constituted by their actualities and potentialities. And indeed it seems [1] obvious that such unities are inseparable from my ego and therefore belong to his concreteness itself.

But what about other egos, who surely are not a mere intending and intended *in me*, merely synthetic unities of possible verification *in me*, but, according to their sense, precisely *others*? Have we not therefore done transcendental realism an injustice? The doctrine may lack a phenomenological foundation; but essentially it is right in the end, since it / looks for ‹122› a path from the immanency of the ego to the transcendency of the Other. Can we, as phenomenologists, do anything but agree with this and say: "The Nature and the whole world that are

[1] Marginal note: Seems? Is.

constituted 'immanently' in the ego are only my 'ideas' and
have behind them the world that exists in itself. The way to this
world must still be sought."? Accordingly can we avoid saying
likewise: "The very question of the possibility of actually transcendent knowledge — above all, that of the possibility of my
going outside my ego and reaching other egos (who, after all, as
others, are not actually in me but only consciously intended in
me) — this question cannot be asked purely phenomenologically"? Is it not *self-understood* from the very beginning that my
field of transcendental knowledge does not reach beyond my
sphere of transcendental experience and what is synthetically
comprised therein? Is it not self-understood that all of that is
included without residue in my own transcendental ego?

But perhaps there is some mistake in thoughts like these.
Before one decides in favor of them and the "self-understood"
propositions they exploit, and then perchance embarks on dialectical argumentations and self-styled "metaphysical" hypotheses (whose supposed possibility may turn out to be complete
absurdity), it might indeed be more fitting to undertake the *task
of phenomenological explication* indicated in this connexion by
the "alter ego" and carry it through in concrete work. We must,
after all, obtain for ourselves insight into the explicit and implicit intentionality wherein the alter ego becomes evinced and
verified in the realm of our transcendental ego; we must discover
in what intentionalities, syntheses, motivations, the sense
"other ego" becomes fashioned in me [1] and, under the title,
harmonious experience of someone else, becomes verified as
existing and even as itself there in its own manner. These experiences and their works are facts belonging to my [2] phenomenological sphere. How else than by examining them can I explicate the sense, existing others, in all its aspects?

§ 43. *The noematic-ontic mode of givenness of the Other,
as transcendental clue for the constitutional theory
of the experience of someone else.*

‹123›   First of all, / my "transcendental clue" is the experienced
Other, given to me in straightforward consciousness and as I

1 The phrase rendered by "in me" crossed out.
2 The word rendered as "belonging to my" crossed out. Marginal comment: "The
dangerous first person singular! This should be expanded terminologically."

immerse myself in examining the noematic-ontic content belonging to him (purely as correlate of my cogito, the particular structure of which is yet to be uncovered). By its remarkableness and multiplicity, that content already indicates the many-sidedness and difficulty of the phenomenological task. For example: In changeable harmonious multiplicities of experience I experience others as actually existing and, on the one hand, as world Objects — not as mere physical things belonging to Nature, though indeed as such things in respect of one side of them. They are in fact experienced also as *governing psychically* in their respective natural organisms [1]. Thus peculiarly involved with animate organisms, as "psychophysical" Objects, they are *"in" the world*. On the other hand, I experience them at the same time as *subjects for this world*, as experiencing it (this same world that I experience) and, in so doing, experiencing me too, even as I experience the world and others in it. Continuing along this line, I can explicate a variety of other moments noematically.

In any case then, within myself, within the limits of my transcendentally reduced pure conscious life, I *experience* the world (including others) — and, according to its experiential sense, *not* as (so to speak) my *private* synthetic formation but as other than mine alone [*mir fremde*], as an *intersubjective* world, actually there for everyone, accessible in respect of its Objects to everyone. And yet each has his experiences, his appearances and appearance-unities, his world-phenomenon; whereas the experienced world exists in itself, over against all experiencing subjects and their world-phenomena.

What is the explanation of this? Imperturbably I must hold fast to the insight that every sense that any existent whatever has or can have for me — in respect of its "what" and its "it exists and actually is" — is a sense *in* and *arising from* my intentional life, becoming clarified and uncovered for me in consequence of my life's constitutive syntheses, in systems of harmonious verification. Therefore, in order to provide the basis for answering all imaginable questions that can have any sense ‹here › — nay, in order that, step by step, these questions themselves may be propounded and solved — it is necessary to begin with a systematic explication of the overt and implicit

This sentence crossed out. Three exclamation points in the margin.

intentionality in which the being of others for me becomes "made" and explicated in respect of its rightful content — that is, its fulfilment-content.

Thus the problem is stated at first as a special one, namely /
<124> that of the "thereness-for-me" of others, and accordingly as the theme of a *transcendental theory of experiencing someone else*, a transcendental theory of so-called "empathy". But it soon becomes evident that the range of such a theory is much greater than at first it seems, that it contributes to the founding of a *transcendental theory of the Objective world* and, indeed, to the founding of such a theory in every respect, notably as regards Objective Nature. The existence-sense [*Seinssinn*] of the world and of Nature in particular, as Objective Nature, includes after all, as we have already mentioned, thereness-for-everyone. This is always cointended whereever we speak of Objective actuality. In addition, Objects with "spiritual" predicates belong to the experienced world. These Objects, in respect of their origin and sense, refer us to subjects, usually other subjects, and their actively constituting intentionality. Thus it is in the case of all cultural Objects (books, tools, works of any kind, and so forth), which moreover carry with them at the same time the experiential sense of thereness-for-everyone (that is, everyone belonging to the corresponding cultural community, such as the European or perhaps, more narrowly, the French cultural community, and so forth).

§ 44. *Reduction of transcendental experience to the sphere of ownness.*

If the transcendental constitution of other subjects and accordingly the transcendental sense, "other subjects", are in question, and consequently a universal sense-stratum [1] that emanates from others [2] and is indispensable to the possibility of an Objective world for me is also in question, then the sense, "other subjects", that is in question here cannot as yet be the

---

[1] Reading, with Typescript C, "*Sinnesschichte*" instead of "*Sinngeschichte*" (sense history).
[2] Reading "*ihnen*" (them) instead of "*innen*" (within), as in both the published text and Typescript C.

sense: "Objective subjects, subjects existing in the world". As regards method, a prime requirement for proceeding correctly here is that first of all we carry out, *inside the universal transcendental sphere, a peculiar kind of epoché* with respect to our theme. For the present we exclude from the thematic field everything now in question: we *disregard all constitutional effects of intentionality relating immediately or mediately to other subjectivity* and delimit first of all the total nexus of that actual and potential intentionality in which the ego constitutes *within himself a peculiar owness* [1]. /

This *reduction to my transcendental sphere of peculiar owness* ⟨125⟩ or to my transcendental concrete I-myself, by abstraction from everything that transcendental constitution gives me as Other, has an unusual sense. In the natural, the world-accepting attitude, I find differentiated and contrasted: myself and others. If I "abstract" (in the usual sense) from others, *I "alone"* remain. But such abstraction is not radical; such aloneness in no respect alters the natural world-sense, "experienceable by everyone", which attaches to the naturally understood Ego and would not be lost, even if a universal plague had left only me. Taken however in the transcendental attitude and at the same time with the constitutional abstraction that we have just characterized, my (the meditator's) ego in his transcendental owness is not the usual I, this man, reduced to a mere correlate phenomenon and having his status within the total world-phenomenon. What concerns us is, on the contrary, *an essential structure, which is part of the all-embracing constitution* in which the transcendental ego, as constituting an Objective world, lives his life.[2]

[1] Originally: constitutes himself in his peculiar owness and synthetic unities inseparable from his peculiar owness, which are therefore to be accounted as part of it.

The following comment was appended later:

§ 44. "inside the universal transcendental sphere" — "peculiar epoché". But it is misleading when the text goes on to say: "in that we exclude from the theoretical ⟨sic⟩ field everything now in question, in that we ⟨disregard⟩ all constitutional effects that relate immediately or mediately to other subjectivity," etc.

The question after all concerns, not other men, but the manner in which the ego (as the transcendental onlooker experiences him transcendentally) constitutes within himself the distinction between Ego and Other Ego — a difference, however, that presents itself first of all in the phenomenon, "world": as the difference between my human Ego (my Ego in the usual sense) and the other human Ego (the other Ego ⟨likewise in the usual sense⟩).

[2] Strasser attaches here the following note, which Husserl wrote on a separate sheet:

What is specifically peculiar to me as ego, my concrete being as a monad, purely in myself and for myself *with an exclusive ownness*, includes <my> every intentionality and therefore, in particular, the intentionality directed to what is other [1]; but, for reasons of method, the synthetic effect of such intentionality (the actuality for me of what is other) shall at first remain excluded from the theme. In this pre-eminent intentionality there becomes constituted for me the new existence-sense that goes beyond my monadic very-ownness; there becomes constituted an ego, not as "I myself", but as mirrored in my own Ego, in my monad. The second ego, however, is not simply there and [2] strictly presented; rather is he constituted as "alter ego" — the ego indicated as one moment by this expression being I myself in my ownness. The "Other", according to his own constituted sense, points to me myself; the other is a "mirroring" of my own self and yet not a mirroring proper, an analogue of my own self and yet again not an analogue in the usual sense. Accordingly <126> if, as / a first step, the ego in his peculiar ownness has been delimited, has been surveyed and articulated in respect of his constituents — not only in the way of life-processes but also in the way of accepted unities concretely inseparable from him —, the question must then be asked: *How* can my ego, within his peculiar ownness, constitute under the name, "experience of something other", precisely something *other* — something, that is, with a sense that excludes the constituted from the concrete make-up of the sense-constituting I-myself, as somehow the latter's analogue? In the first place the question concerns no matter what alter egos; then however it concerns everything that acquires sense-determinations from them — in short, an Objective world in the proper and full signification of the phrase.

The total appearance of the world — the world always intended in the flux.
The total appearance of Nature.
The total intending of the world, the particular intending — the particular appearance of the particular wordly object. But the intending has strata; I can abstract. Physical-thing appearance, stratum of culture or stratum of human existence as <blank-space> in the flowing present. The stream of world-"appearances", of "perceptual appearances"; what is intended ontologically. Cogito-strata, such that each stratum has a stratum of the cogitatum. The ego directed to what is intended.
[1] Marginal comment: ?! To men and to myself as a man.
[2] Reading, with Typescript C, "und" instead of "uns" (to us).

These problems will become more understandable if we proceed to characterize the ego's sphere of owness or, correlatively,
to carry out explicitly the abstractive epoché that yields it.
Thematic exclusion of the constitutional effects produced by
experience of something other, together with the effects of
all the further modes of consciousness relating to something
other, does not signify merely phenomenological epoché with
respect to naïve acceptance of the being of the other, as in the
case of everything Objective existing for us in straightforward
consciousness. After all, the transcendental attitude is and
remains presupposed, the attitude according to which everything previously existing for us in straightforward consciousness
is taken exclusively as "phenomenon", as a sense meant and
undergoing verification, purely in the manner in which, as correlate of uncoverable constitutive systems, it has gained and is
gaining existential sense. We are now preparing for just this
uncovering and sense-clarification by the novel epoché, more
particularly in the following manner.

As Ego in the transcendental attitude I attempt first of all to
delimit, within my horizon of transcendental experience, *what
is peculiarly my own*. First I say that it is *non-alien* [*Nicht-
Fremdes*]. I begin by freeing that horizon abstractively from
everything that is at all alien. A property of the transcendental
phenomenon "world" is that of being given in harmonious
straightforward experience; accordingly it is necessary to survey
this world and pay attention to how something alien makes its
appearance as jointly determining the sense of the world and,
so far as it does so, to exclude it abstractively. Thus we abstract
first of all from what gives men and brutes their specific sense
as, so to speak, Ego-like living beings and / consequently from ‹127›
all determinations of the phenomenal world that refer by their
sense to "others" as Ego-subjects and, accordingly, presuppose
these. For example, all cultural predicates. We can say also that
we abstract from everything *"other-spiritual"*, as that which
makes possible, in the "alien" or "other" that is in question
here, its specific sense. Furthermore the *characteristic of belonging
to the surrounding world*, not merely for others who are also
given at the particular time in actual experience, but also *for
everyone*, the characteristic of being there for and accessible to

everyone, of being capable of mattering or not mattering to each in his living and striving, — a characteristic of all Objects belonging to the phenomenal world and the characteristic wherein their otherness consists — should not be overlooked, but rather excluded abstractively.

In this connexion we note something important. When we thus abstract, *we retain a unitarily coherent stratum of the phenomenon world*, a stratum of the phenomenon that is the correlate of continuously harmonious, continuing world-experience. *Despite* our abstraction, we can *go on continuously in our experiencing intuition*, while remaining exclusively in the aforesaid stratum. This unitary stratum, furthermore, is distinguished by being essentially the *founding* stratum — that is to say: I obviously cannot have the "alien" or "other" as experience, and therefore cannot have the sense "Objective world" as an experiential sense, without having this stratum in actual experience; whereas the reverse is not the case.

Let us observe more closely the result of our abstraction and, accordingly, what it leaves us. From the phenomenon world, from the world appearing with an Objective sense, a substratum becomes separated, as the *"Nature" included in my ownness*, a Nature that must always be carefully distinguished from Nature, pure and simple — that is to say: from the Nature that becomes the theme of the natural scientist. *This* Nature, to be sure, is likewise a result of abstraction, namely abstraction from everything psychic and from those predicates of the Objective world that have arisen from persons. But what is acquired by this abstraction on the part of the natural scientist is a stratum that belongs to the Objective world itself (viewed in the transcendental attitude, a stratum that belongs to the *objective sense:* "Objective world") and is therefore itself Objective — just as, on the other hand, what is abstracted *from* is Objective (the Objective psychic, Objective cultural predicates, and so forth). But in the case of *our* abstraction the sense "Objective", which belongs to everything worldly — as constituted intersubjectively, <128> as / experienceable by everyone, and so forth — *vanishes completely*. Thus there is included in my ownness, as purified from every sense pertaining to other subjectivity, *a sense, "mere Nature"*, that has lost precisely that "by everyone" and therefore must not by any means be taken for an abstract stratum of the world or of the world's sense. Among the bodies belonging to this "Nature" and included in my peculiar ownness, I then find my *animate organism* as *uniquely* singled out — namely as the only one of them that is not just a body but precisely an animate organism: the sole Object within my abstract world-stratum to which, in accordance with experience, I ascribe *fields of sensation* (belonging to it, however, in different manners — a field of tactual sensations, a field of warmth and coldness, and so forth), the only Object "in" which I *"rule and govern"* *immediately*, governing particularly in each of its "organs". Touching kinesthetically, I perceive "with" my hands; seeing kinesthetically, I perceive also "with" my eyes; and so forth; moreover I can perceive thus at any time. Meanwhile the *kinesthesias* pertaining to the organs flow in the mode "I am doing", and are subject to my "I can"; furthermore, by calling these kinesthesias into play, I can push, thrust, and so forth, and can thereby *"act"* *somatically* — immediately, and then mediately. As *perceptively* active, *I experience* (or can experience) *all of Nature, including my own animate organism*, which therefore in the process is reflexively related to itself. That becomes possible because I "can" perceive one hand "by means of" the other, an eye by means of a hand, and so forth — a procedure in which *the functioning organ must become an Object and the Object a functioning organ*. And it is the same in the case of my generally possible original *dealing* with Nature and with my animate organism itself, by means of this organism — which therefore is reflexively related to itself *also in practice*.

Bringing to light my animate organism, reduced to what is included in my ownness, is itself part of bringing to light the *ownness-essence* of the Objective phenoemnon: *"I, as this man"*. If I reduce *other* men to what is included in my ownness, I get *bodies* included therein; if I reduce *myself* as a man, I get *"my animate organism"* and *"my psyche"*, or myself as a *psychophysical unity* — *in the latter, my personal Ego*, who operates in tihs animate organism and, "by means of" it, in the *"external world"*, who is affected by this world, and who thus in all respects, by virtue of the continual experience of such unique modes of Ego- and life-relatedness, is constituted as psychophysically

united with the animate corporeal organism. If *ownness-purie*
‹129› *fication of the external world, the animate organism, / and th-*
psychophysical whole, has been effected, I have lost my natural
sense as Ego, since every sense-relation to a possible Us or We
remains excluded, and have lost likewise all my worldliness, in
the natural sense. But, in my spiritual ownness, I am nevertheless the identical Ego-pole of my manifold "pure" subjective
processes, those of my passive and active intentionality, and the
pole of all the habitualities instituted or to be instituted by those
processes.

Accordingly this peculiar abstractive sense-exclusion of what
is alien leaves us a *kind of "world"* still, a Nature reduced to
what is included in our ownness and, as having its place in this
Nature thanks to the bodily organism, the psychophysical Ego,
with "body and soul" and personal Ego — utterly *unique*
members of this reduced "world". Manifestly predicates that
get significance from *this* Ego also occur in the reduced world —
for example: "value" predicates and predicates of "works" as
such. None of this is worldly in the natural sense (therefore all
the quotation-marks); it is all exclusively what is mine in my
world-experience, pervading my world-experience through and
through and likewise cohering unitarily in my intuition. Accordingly the members we distinguish in this, my peculiarly
own world-phenomenon, are *concretely* united, as is further
shown by the fact that the *spatiotemporal form* — as reduced,
however, to the form included in my ownness — also goes into
this reduced world-phenomenon. Hence the reduced "Objects"
— the "physical things", the "psychophysical Ego" — are
likewise *outside one another.*

But here something remarkable strikes us: a sequence of evidences that yet, *in* their sequence, seem paradoxical. The
psychic life of my Ego (this "psychophysical" Ego), including
my whole world-experiencing life and therefore including my
actual and possible experience *of* what is other, is wholly unaffected by screening off what is other. Consequently there belongs
within my psychic being the whole constitution of the world
existing for me and, in further consequence, the differentiation
of that constitution into the systems that constitute what is
included in my peculiar ownness and the systems that constitute

what is other. I, the reduced "human Ego" ("psychophysical" Ego), am constituted, accordingly, as a member of the "world" with a multiplicity of "objects outside me". But I myself constitute all this in my "psyche" and bear it intentionally within me. If perchance it could be shown that everything constituted as part of my peculiar ownness, including then the reduced "world", / belonged to the concrete essence of the constituting subject as ‹130› an inseparable internal determination, then, in the Ego's self-explication, his peculiarly own world would be found as "inside" and, on the other hand, when running through that world straightforwardly, the Ego would find himself as a member among its "externalities" and would distinguish between himself and "the external world".

§ 45. *The transcendental ego, and self-apperception as a psychophysical man reduced to what is included in my ownness.*

These last meditations, like all the others, have been carried on by us in the attitude that effects transcendental reduction — carried on, that is to say, by me (the meditator) as transcendental ego. We now ask how I, the human Ego reduced to what is purely my own and, as thus reduced, included in the similarly reduced world-phenomenon and, on the other hand, I as transcendental ego are related to one another. The transcendental ego emerged by virtue of my "parenthesizing" of the entire Objective world and all other (including all ideal) Objectivities. In consequence of this parenthesizing, I have become aware of myself as the transcendental ego, who constitutes in his constitutive life everything that is ever Objective for me — the ego of all constitutions, who exists in his actual and potential life-processes and Ego-habitualities and who constitutes in them not only everything Objective but also himself as identical ego. We can say now: In that I, as this ego, have constituted and am continually further constituting as a phenomenon [1] (as a correlate) the world that exists for me, I have carried out a *mundanizing self-apperception* — under the title "Ego in the usual sense" — in corresponding constitutive syntheses and am maintaining a

[1] The phrase "as a phenomenon" supplied in accordance with Typescript C and the French translation.

continuing acceptance and further development of it. By virtue of this mundanization everything included in the ownness belonging to me transcendentally (as this ultimate ego) enters, as something *psychic*, into "my psyche". I find the mundanizing apperception; and now, from the psyche as phenomenon and part of the phenomenon man, I can go back to the all-inclusive *absolute* ego, the *transcendental* ego. Therefore if I, as this ego, reduce my phenomenon, "the Objective world", to what is included in my peculiar ownness and take in addition whatever else I find as peculiarly my *own* (which can no longer contain anything "alien" or "other", after that reduction), then all this ownness of my ego is to be found again, in the reduced world-phenomenon, as the ownness / of *"my psyche"*. Here, however, as a component pertaining to my world-apperception, it is something *transcendentally secondary*. Restricting ourselves to the ultimate transcendental ego and the universe of what is constituted in him, we can say that a division of his whole transcendental field of experience belongs to him immediately, namely the division into the sphere of his ownness — with the coherent stratum consisting in his experience of a world reduced to what is included in his ownness [1] (an experience in which everything "other" is "screened off") — and the sphere of what is "other". Yet every *consciousness of* what is other, every mode of appearance *of* it, belongs in the former sphere. Whatever the transcendental ego constitutes in that *first* stratum, whatever he constitutes as non-other, as his "peculiarly own" — that indeed belongs to him as *a component of his own concrete essence* (as we shall show); it is inseparable from his concrete being. Within and by means of this ownness the transcendental ego constitutes, however, the "Objective" world, as a universe of being that is other than himself — and constitutes, at the first level, the other in the mode: alter ego.

‹131›

§ 46. *Ownness as the sphere of the actualities and potentialities of the stream of subjective processes.*

Up to now we have characterized the fundamental concept of "my own" only indirectly: as *non-alien* or *non-other* — a charac-

---

[1] The phrase "reduced to what is included in his ownness" supplied in accordance with Typescript C and the French translation.

terization that is based on, and thus presupposes, the concept of another ego. In order to clarify the sense of this "my own" it is important, however, to bring out its positive characteristic, or the positive characteristic of "the ego in his [1] ownness". This characteristic was merely indicated in the last sentences of the preceding section.

As our point of departure let us take something more general. If a concrete object stands out for us in experience as something particular, and our attentively grasping regard then becomes directed to it, it becomes appropriated in this simple grasping merely as "an undetermined object of empirical intuition". It becomes a determined object, and one undergoing further determination, in a continuation of the experience in the form of a determining experience, which at first unfolds only what is included in the object itself: a pure *explication*. In its articulated synthetic course, on the basis of the object given as self-identical in a continuous intuitive synthesis of identification, this pure explication unfolds, in a concatenation of particular intuitions the object's very / own determinations, the "internal" determi- ᐳ 132ᐳ nations. These present themselves originaliter as determinations *in* which it, the Identical itself, is [2] what it is and, moreover, exists in itself, "in and of itself" — determinations wherein its identical being becomes explicated as the particulars making up its ownness: what it is, in particular. This own-essential content is only generally and horizonally anticipated beforehand; it then becomes constituted originaliter — with the sense: internal, own-essential feature (specifically, part or property) — by explication.

Let us apply this. When I am effecting transcendental reduction and reflecting on myself, the transcendental ego, I am given to myself *perceptually* as this ego — in a grasping perception. Furthermore I become aware that, although not grasped before this perception, I was "already given", already there for myself continually as an object of original intuition (as perceived in the broader sense). But I am given, in any case, with an open infinite horizon of still undiscovered *internal features of my own*.

---

[1] Reading "*seiner*" instead of "*meiner*" (my), as in both the published text and Typescript C.

[2] Supplied in accordance with Typescript C and the French translation

My own too is discovered by explication and gets its original sense by virtue thereof. It becomes uncovered originaliter when my experiencing-explicating regard is directed to myself, to my perceptually and even apodictically given "I am" and its abiding identity with itself [1] in the continuous unitary synthesis of original self-experience. Whatever is included in this identical being's own essence is characterized as its actual or possible explicatum, as a respect in which I merely unfold my own identical being as what it, as identical, is in particular: it in itself.

Now the following is to be noted here. Though I speak rightly of *self-perception*, and indeed as regards my concrete ego, that is not to say that, like explication of a perceptually given "visual thing", self-explication always goes on in particular *perceptions*, in the proper sense, and accordingly yields just perceptual explicata and no others. After all, when explicating the horizon of being that is included in my own essence, one of the first things I run into is my immanent temporality and, with it, my existence in the form of an open infiniteness, that of a stream of subjective processes, and in the form of all those "ownnesses" of mine that are somehow included in the stream — one of which is my explicating. Since it goes on in the living present, self-explication ‹133› can / find, strictly *perceptively*, only what is going on in the living present. In the most original manner conceivable it uncovers my own past by means of recollections. Therefore, though I am continually given to myself originaliter and can explicate progressively what is included in my own essence, this explication is *carried out largely in acts of consciousness that are not perceptions* of the own-essential moments it discovers. Thus alone can my stream of subjective processes, the stream in which I live as the identical Ego, become accessible to me: first of all, in respect of its actualities, and then in respect of the potentialities that manifestly are likewise moments of my own essence. All possibilities of the kind subsumed under the I "can" or "could have" set this or that series of subjective processes going (including in particular: I can look ahead or look back, I can penetrate and uncover the horizon of my temporal being) — all such possibilities manifestly belong to me as moments of my own essence.

In every case, however, explication is original if, precisely on

---

[1] According to Typescript C: "and my abiding identity with myself".

the basis of original self-experience, it unfolds the experienced itself and confers upon the experienced that self-giveness which is, for it, the *most original conceivable*. The *apodictic evidence* of transcendental self-perception (the apodictic evidence of the "I am") extends into such explication, though with a previously stated *restriction*. In unqualifiedly apodictic evidence self-explication brings out only the all-embracing structural forms in which I exist as ego — that is to say: in which I exist with an essentially necessary all-inclusiveness and without which I could not exist. They include (among others) the mode of existence in the form of a certain all-embracing life of some sort or other, that of existence in the form of the continuous self-constitution of that life's own processes, as temporal within an all-embracing time, and so forth. In this *all-embracing apodictic Apriori*, with its undetermined universality and, on the other hand, its determinability, every explication of single egological data then participates — for example: as a certain, albeit imperfect, evidence contained in the recollection of my own past. The participation in apodicticity appears in the *formal law* (which is itself apodictic): So much illusion, so much being — which is only covered up and falsified thereby and which therefore can be asked about, sought, and (by following a predelineated way) found, even if only with approximation to its fully determined content. This fully determined content itself, with the sense of something firmly identifiable again and again, in respect of all its parts and moments, is an "idea", valid a priori. /

§ 47. *The intentional object also belongs to the full monadic* <134> *concretion of ownness. Immanent transcendence and primordial world.*

Manifestly (and this is of particular importance) the own-essentiaaliy belonging to me as ego comprises more than merely the pctualities and potentialities of the stream of subjective rtocesses. Just as it comprises the constitutive systems, *it comprises the constituted unities* — but with a certain *restriction*. That is to say: Where, and *so far as, the constituted unity is inseparable from the original constitution itself*, with the inseparableness that characterizes an immediate [1] *concrete* oneness, not only the constitutive perceiving but also the perceived existent belongs to my concrete very-ownness.

That is not only the case with sensuous data, which, taken as mere data of sensation, become constituted as peculiarly my own: as *"immanent temporalities"* within the limits of my ego. It is also the case with all my *habitualities*, which are likewise peculiarly my own: the habitualities that begin with institutive acts of my own and become constituted as abiding convictions in which *I myself* become abidingly convinced of such and such, and by virtue of which I, as polar Ego (Ego in the particular sense: mere Ego-pole), acquire determinations that are specifically Ego-determinations. But *"transcendent objects"* (for example: the objects of *"external"* sensuousness, unities belonging to multiplicites of sensuous modes of appearance) also belong here: if I, as ego, take into account just what is constituted *actually originaliter* as an appearing spatial object by my own sensuousness, my own apperceptions, *as itself concretely inseparable from them*. We see forthwith that the *entire reduced "world"*, which we previously obtained by excluding the sense-components pertaining to what is other or alien, belongs in this sphere and is rightly included in the positively defined concrete make-up of the ego: as something peculiarly his *own*. As soon as we exclude from consideration the intentional effects produced by "empathy", by our experience of others, we have a Nature (including an animate organism) that is constituted, to be sure, as a unity of spatial objects "transcending" the stream of subjective processes, yet constituted as merely a multiplicity of ‹135› objects / of possible experience — this experience being purely *my own* life, and what is experienced in this experience being nothing more than a synthetic unity inseparable from this life and its potentialities.

In this manner it becomes clear that *the ego, taken concretely*, has a *universe of what is peculiarly his own*, which can be uncovered by an original explication of his apodictic "ego sum" — an explication that is itself apodictic or at least predelineative of an apodictic form. *Within* this *"original sphere"* (the sphere

---

[1] Reading *"unmittelbarer"* instead of *"unmittelbar"* (immediately), as in both the published text and Typescript C. Cf. the French: *"immédiate et concrète"*.

of original self-explication) we find also a "transcendent world", which accrues on the basis of the intentional phenomenon, "Objective world", by reduction to what is peculiarly the ego's own (in the positive sense, which is now preferred). But, provided only that they are subjected to our reduction to what is included in the ego's ownness, all the corresponding illusions, phantasies, "pure" possibilities, and eidetic objectivities, which offer themselves as "transcendent", likewise belong in this domain — the domain of my peculiarly own essentiality, of what I am in myself, in my full concreteness or (as we may also say) what I am in myself as this monad [1].

§ 48. *The transcendency of the Objective world as belonging to a level higher than that of primordial transcendency.*

That my own essence can be at all contrasted for me with something else, or that I (who am I) can become aware of someone else (who is not I but someone other than I), presupposes that *not all my own modes of consciousness are modes of my self-consciousness*. Since actual being is constituted originally by harmoniousness of experience, my own self must contain, in contrast to self-experience and the system of its harmoniousness (the system, therefore, of self-explication into components of my ownness), yet other experiences united in harmonious systems. And now the *problem* is how we are to understand the fact that the ego has, and can always go on forming, in himself such intentionalities of a different kind, intentionalities with an existence-sense whereby *he wholly transcends his own being*. How can something actually existent for me — and, as that, not just somehow meant but undergoing harmonious verification in me — be anything else than, so to speak, a point of intersection belonging to my constitutive synthesis? As concretely inseparable from my synthesis, is it peculiarly my own? But even the / possibility of a vaguest, emptiest intending of something alien ‹136› is problematic, if it is true that, essentially, every such mode of consciousness involves its possibilities of an uncovering of what is intended, its possibilities of becoming converted into either

---

[1] Reading with Typescript C and the French translation. According to the published text: "or (as we may also say) in my monad".

fulfilling or disillusioning experiences of what is meant, and moreover, (as regards the genesis of the consciousness) points back to such experiences of the same intended object or a similar one.

The fact of experience of something alien (something that is not I), is present as experience of an Objective world and others in it (non-Ego in the form: other Ego); and an important result of the owness-reduction performed on these experiences was that it brought out a substratum belonging to them, an intentional substratum in which a reduced "world" shows itself, as an "immanent transcendency". In the order pertaining to constitution of a world *alien to my Ego* — a world *"external" to my own concrete Ego* (but not at all in the natural spatial sense) — that reduced world is the intrinsically first, the *"primordial" transcendency* (or "world"); and, regardless of its *ideality* as a synthetic unity belonging to an infinite system of my potentialities, it is *still a determining part of my own concrete being*, the being that belongs to me as concrete ego.

It must now be made understandable *how*, at the founded higher level, the sense-bestowal pertaining to transcendency proper, to constitutionally secondary *Objective transcendency*, comes about — and does so as an experience. Here it is not a matter of uncovering a genesis going on in time, but a matter of *"static analysis"*. The Objective world is constantly there before me as already finished, a datum of my livingly continuous Objective experience and, even in respect of what is no longer experienced, something I go on accepting habitually. It is a matter of examining this experience itself and uncovering intentionally the manner in which it bestows sense, the manner in which it can occur as experience and become verified as evidence relating to an actual existent with an explicatable essence of *its* own, which is not *my* own essence and has no place as a constituent part thereof, though it nevertheless can acquire sense and verification only in my essence. /

‹137› § 49. *Predelineation of the course to be followed by intentional explication of experiencing what is other.*

Constitution of the existence-sense, "Objective world", on the basis of my primordial "world", involves a number of levels.

As the *first* of these, there is to be distinguished the constitutional level pertaining to the "other ego" or to any "other egos" whatever — that is: to egos *excluded* from my own concrete being (from me as the "primordial ego"). In connexion with that and, indeed, motivated by it, there occurs a *universal super-addition of sense to my primordial world*, whereby the latter becomes the *appearance "of"* a determinate "Objective" world, as the identical world for everyone, myself included. Accordingly *the intrinsically first other* (the first "non-Ego") *is the other Ego*. And the other Ego makes constitutionally possible a new infinite domain of what is "other": an *Objective Nature* and a whole Objective world, to which all other Egos and I myself belong. This constitution, arising on the basis of the *"pure"* others (the other Egos who as yet have no worldly sense), is essentially such that the "others"-for-me do not remain isolated; on the contrary, an *Ego-community*, which includes me, becomes constituted (in my sphere of ownness, naturally) as a community of Egos existing with each other and for each other — *ultimately a community of monads*, which, moreover, (in its communalized intentionality) constitutes the *one identical world. In this world* all Egos again present themselves, but *in an Objectivating apperception* with the sense *"men"* or "psychophysical men as worldly Objects".

By virtue of the mentioned communalization ‹of constitutive intentionality›, the transcendental intersubjectivity has an *intersubjective* sphere of ownness, in which it constitutes the Objective world; and thus, as the transcendencental "We", it is a subjectivity for this world and also for the world of men, which is the form in which it has made itself Objectively actual. If, however, intersubjective sphere of ownness and Objective world are to be distinguished here, nevertheless, when I as ego take my stand on the basis of the intersubjectivity constituted from sources within my own essence, I can recognize that the Objective world does not, in the proper sense, / *transcend* that ‹138› sphere or that sphere's own intersubjective essence, but rather inheres in it as an "immanent" transcendency. Stated more precisely: The Objective world as an *idea* — the ideal correlate of an intersubjective (intersubjectively communalized) experience, which ideally can be and is carried on as constantly harmonious — is essentially related to intersubjectivity (itself constituted as having the ideality of endless openness), whose component particular subjects are equiped with mutually corresponding and harmonious constitutive systems. Consequently *the constitution of the world essentially involves a "harmony" of the monads:* precisely this harmony among particular constitutions in the particular monads; and accordingly it involves also a harmonious generation that goes on in each particular monad. That is not meant, however, as a "metaphysical" hypothesizing of monadic harmony, any more than the monads themselves are metaphysical inventions or hypotheses. On the contrary, it is itself part of the explication of the intentional components implicit in the fact of the experiential world that exists for us. Here again it is to be noted that, as has been repeatedly emphasized, the ideas referred to are not phantasies or modes of the "as if", but arise constitutionally in integral connexion with all Objective experience and have their modes of legitimation and their development by scientific activity.

What we have just presented is a preliminary view of the course to be followed, level by level, in the intentional explication that we must carry out, if we are to solve the transcendental problem in the only conceivable way and actually execute the transcendental idealism of phenomenology.

§ 50. *The mediate intentionality of experiencing someone else, as "appresentation" (analogical apperception).*

After we have dealt with the prior stage, which is very important transcendentally — namely, definition and articulation of the primordial sphere —, the genuine difficulties (and in fact they are not inconsiderable) are occasioned by the *first* of the above-indicated steps toward constitution of an Objective world: *the step taking us to the "other" ego.* They lie, accordingly, in the transcendental clarification of experiencing "someone else" — in the sense in which the other has not yet attained the sense "man". /

<139> Experience is original consciousness; and in fact we generally say, in the case of experiencing a man: the other is himself there

before us "in person". On the other hand, this being there in person does not keeps us from admitting forthwith that, properly speaking, neither the other Ego himself, nor his subjective processes or his appearances themselves, nor anything else belonging to his own essence, becomes given in our experience originally. If it were, if what belongs to the other's own essence were directly accessible, it would be merely a moment of my own essence, and ultimately he himself and I myself would be the same. The situation would be similar as regards his animate organism, if the latter were nothing else but the "body" that is a unity constituted purely in my actual and possible experiences, a unity belonging — as a product of *my* "sensuousness" exclusively — in my primordial sphere. *A certain mediacy of intentionality* must be present here, going out from the substratum, "primordial world", (which in any case is the incessantly underlying basis) and making present to consciousness a "there too", which nevertheless is not itself there and can never become an "itself-there". We have here, accordingly, a kind of *making "co-present"*, a kind of *"appresentation"*.

An appresentation occurs even in external experience, since the strictly seen front of a physical thing always and necessarily appresents a rear aspect and prescribes for it a more or less determinate content. On the other hand, experiencing someone else cannot be a matter of just this kind of appresentation, which already plays a role in the constitution of primordial Nature: Appresentation of this sort involves the possibility of verification by a corresponding fulfilling presentation (the back becomes the front); whereas, in the case of that appresentation which would lead over into the other original sphere, such verification must be excluded a priori. How can appresentation of another original sphere, and thereby the sense "someone else", be motivated in my original sphere and, in fact, motivated as experience — as the word "appresentation" (making intended as co-present) already indicates? Not every non-originary making-present can do that. A non-originary making-present can do it only in combination with an originary presentation, an itself-giving proper; and only as demanded by the originary presentation can it have the character of appresentation — somewhat as, in the case of experiencing a physical thing, what is there perceptually motivates <belief in > something else being there too.

The perception proper that functions as the underlying basis is
<140> offered us by our / *perception of the primordially reduced world*, with its previously described articulation — a perception going on continually within the general bounds of the ego's *incessant self-perception*. The problem now is: In the perception of that reduced world, what in particular must be of account here? How does the motivation run? What becomes uncovered as involved in the very complicated intentional performance of the appresentation, which does in fact come about?

Initial guidance can be furnished by the verbal sense, *an Other:* an Other Ego. "Alter" signifies alter ego. And the ego involved here is I myself, constituted within my primordial ownness, and uniquely, as the psychophysical unity (the primordial man): as "personal" Ego, governing immediately in my animate organism (the only animate organism) and producing effects mediately [1] in the primordial surrounding world; the subject, moreover, of a concrete intentional life, <and (?) > of a psychic sphere relating to himself and the "world". All of that — with the grouping under types that arises in experiential life and the familiar forms of flow and combination — is at our disposal. As for the intentionalities by which it has become constituted (and they too are highly complicated) — admittedly we have not investigated them <in these meditations >. They belong to a distinct stratum and are the theme of vast investigations into which we did not and could not enter.

Let us assume that another man enters our perceptual sphere. Primordially reduced, that signifies: In the perceptual sphere pertaining to my primordial Nature, a body is presented, which, as primordial, is of course only a determining part of myself: an "immanent transcendency". Since, in this Nature and this world, my animate organism is the only body that is or can be constituted originally as an animate organism (a functioning organ), the body over there, which is nevertheless apprehended as an animate organism, must have derived this sense by an *apperceptive transfer from my animate organism*, and done so in

---

[1] According to the published text, Typescript C and the French translaton: "immediately".

a manner that excludes an actually direct, and hence primordial, showing of the predicates belonging to an animate organism specifically, a showing of them in perception proper. It is clear from the very beginning that only a similarity connecting, within my primordial sphere, that body over there with my body can serve as the motivational basis for the *"analogizing" apprehension* of that body as another animate organism. /

There would be, accordingly, a certain assimilative apperception; but it by no means follows that there would by an inference from analogy. Apperception is not inference, not a thinking act. *Every* apperception in which we apprehend at a glance, and noticingly grasp, objects given beforehand — for example, the already-given everyday world — every apperception in which we understand their sense and its horizons forthwith, points back to a *"primal instituting"*, in which an object with a similar sense became constituted for the first time. Even the physical things of this world that are unknown to us are, to speak generally, known in respect of their type. We have already seen like things before, though not precisely this thing here. Thus *each everyday experience* involves an *analogizing transfer* of an originally instituted objective sense to a new case, with its anticipative apprehension of the object as having a similar sense. To the extent that there is givenness beforehand, there is such a transfer. At the same time, that sense-component in further experience which proves to be actually new may function in turn as institutive and found a pregivenness that has a richer sense. The child who already sees physical things understands, let us say, for the first time the final sense of scissors; and from now on he sees scissors at the first glance *as* scissors — but naturally not in an explicit reproducing, comparing, and inferring. Yet the manner in which apperceptions arise — and consequently in themselves, by their sense and sense-horizon, point back to their genesis — varies greatly. There are different levels of apperception, corresponding to different layers of objective sense. Ultimately we always get back to the *radical differentiation of apperceptions* into those that, according to their genesis, belong purely to the *primordial sphere* and those that present themselves *with the sense "alter ego"* and, *upon* this sense, have built a new one — thanks to a genesis at a higher level.

‹141›

§ 51. *"Pairing" as an associatively constitutive component of my experience of someone else.*

If we attempt to indicate the peculiar nature of that analogizing apprehension whereby a body within my primordial sphere, being similar to my own animate body, becomes *apprehended as likewise an animate organism*, we encounter: first, the ‹142› circumstance that here the *primally institutive original* / is *always livingly present*, and the primal instituting itself is therefore always going on in a livingly effective manner; secondly, the peculiarity we already know to be necessary, namely that what is *appresented* by virtue of the aforesaid analogizing can never attain actual presence, never become an object of perception proper. Closely connected with the first peculiarity is the circumstance that *ego* and *alter ego* are always and necessarily given *in an original "pairing"*.

Pairing, occurence in configuration as a pair and then as a group, a plurality, is a *universal* phenomenon of the transcendental sphere (and of the parallel sphere of intentional psychology); and, we may add forthwith, as far as a pairing is actually present, so far extends that remarkable kind of primal instituting of an analogizing apprehension — its continuous primal institution in living actuality — which we have already stressed as the first peculiarity of experiencing someone else. Hence it is not exclusively peculiar to this experience.

First of all, let us elucidate the essential nature of any "pairing" (or any forming of a plurality). Pairing is a *primal form of that passive synthesis* which we designate as *"association"*, in contrast to passive synthesis of "identification". In a *pairing association* the characteristic feature is that, in the most primitive case, two data are given intuitionally, and with prominence, in the unity of a consciousness and that, on this basis — essentially, already in pure passivity (regardless therefore of whether they are noticed or unnoticed) —, as data appearing with mutual distinctness, they *found phenomenologically a unity of similarity* and thus are always constituted precisely as a pair. If there are more than two such data, then a phenomenally unitary group, a plurality, becomes constituted. On more precise analysis we find essentially present here an intentional overreaching, coming about genetically (and by essential necessity) as soon as the data that undergo pairing have become prominent and simultaneously intended; we find, more particularly, a living mutual awakening and an overlaying of each with the objective sense of the other. This overlaying can bring a total or a partial coincidence, which in any particular instance has its degree, the limiting case being that of complete "likeness". As the result of this overlaying, there takes place in the paired data a mutual transfer of sense — that is to say: an apperception of each according to the sense of the other, so far as / moments of sense actualized in what is ‹143› experienced do not annul this transfer, with the consciousness of "different".

In that case of association and apperception which particularly interests us — namely apperception of the alter ego by the ego — pairing first comes about when the Other enters my field of perception. I, as the primordial psychophysical Ego, am always prominent in my primordial field of perception, regardless of whether I pay attention to myself and turn toward myself with some activity or other In particular, my live body is always there and sensuously prominent; but, in addition to that and likewise with primordial originariness, it is equipped with the specific sense of an animate organism. Now in case there presents itself, as outstanding in my primordial sphere, a body "similar" to mine — that is to say, a body with determinations such that it must enter into a phenomenal *pairing* with mine — it *seems* clear without more ado that, with the transfer of sense, this body must forthwith appropriate from mine the sense: animate organism. But is the apperception actually so transparent? Is it a simple apperception by transfer, like any other? What makes this organism another's, rather than a second organism of my own? Obviously what we designated as the *second fundamental characteristic* of the apperception in question plays a part here: that none of the *appropriated* sense specific to an animate organism can become actualized originarily in my primordial sphere.

§ 52. *Appresentation as a kind of experience with its own style of verification.*

But now there arises for us the difficult problem of making it understandable *that such an apperception is possible* and need not be annulled forthwith. How does it happen that, as the fact tells us, the transferred sense is appropriated with existence-status, as a set of "psychic" determinations existing in combination with that body over there, even though they can never show themselves *as* themselves in the domain of originality, belonging to the primordial sphere (which alone is available)?

Let us look at the intentional situation more closely. The appresentation which gives that component of the Other which is not accessible originaliter is combined with an original presentation (of "his" body as part of the Nature given as included in my ownness). In this combination, moreover, the Other's ‹144› animate body and his governing Ego / are given in the manner that characterizes *a unitary transcending experience.* Every experience points to further experiences that would fulfil and verify the appresented horizons, which include, in the form of non-intuitive anticipations, potentially verifiable syntheses of harmonious further experience. Regarding experience of someone else, it is clear that its fulfillingly verifying continuation can ensue *only by means of new appresentations that proceed in a synthetically harmonious fashion,* and only by virtue of the manner in which *these appresentations owe their existence-value to their motivational connexion with the* changing *presentations proper, within my ownness,* that continually appertain to them.

As a suggestive *clue* to the requisite clarification, this proposition may suffice: The experienced animate organism of another continues to prove itself as actually an animate organism, solely in its changing but incessantly *harmonious "behavior".* Such *harmonious* behavior (as having a physical side that indicates something psychic appresentatively) must present itself fulfillingly in original experience, and do so throughout the continuous change in behavior from phase to phase. The organism becomes experienced as a pseudo-organism, precisely if there is something discordant about its behavior.

The character of the existent "other" has its basis in this kind of verifiable accessibility of what is not originally accessible. Whatever can become presented, and evidently verified, *originally* — is something *I* am; or else it belongs to me as peculiarly my own. Whatever, by virtue thereof, is experienced in that founded manner which characterizes a primordially unfulfillable

experience — an experience that does not give something itself
originally but that consistently verifies something indicated —
is "other". It is therefore conceivable only as an analogue of
something included in my peculiar ownness. Because of its sense-
constitution it occurs necessarily as an *"intentional modification"*
of that Ego of mine which is the first to be Objectivated, or as
an intentional modification of my primordial "world": the
Other as phenomenologically a "modification" of myself (which,
for its part, gets this character of being "my" self by virtue of
the contrastive pairing that necessarily takes place). It is clear
that, with the other Ego, there is appresented, in an analogizing
modification, everything that belongs to his concretion: first,
his primordial world, and then his fully concrete ego. In other
words, *another monad* becomes constituted appresentatively in
mine.

Similarly (to draw an instructive comparison), within my
ownness and moreover within / the sphere of its living present, ‹145›
my past is given only by memory and is characterized in memory
as my past, a past present — that is: an intentional modification. The experiential verification of it, as a modification, then
goes on necessarily in harmonious syntheses of recollection; only
thus does a past as such become verified. Somewhat as my
memorial past, as a modification of my living present, "transcends" my present, the appresented other being "transcends"
my own being (in the pure and most fundamental sense: what
is included in my primordial ownness). In both cases the modification is inherent as a sense-component in the sense itself; it is
a correlate of the intentionality constituting it. Just as, in my
living present, in the domain of "internal perception", my past
becomes constituted by virtue of the harmonious memories
occuring in this present, so in my primordial sphere, by means
of appresentations occuring in it and motivated by its contents,
an ego other than mine can become constituted — accordingly,
in non-originary presentations [*in Vergegenwärtigungen*] of a
new type, which have a modificatum of a new kind as their
correlate. To be sure, as long as I consider non-originary presentations ‹of something lying› within the sphere of my ownness,
the Ego in whom they center is the one identical I-myself. On
the other hand, to everything alien (as long as it remains whitin

the appresented horizon of concreteness that necessarily goes with it) centers in an appresented Ego who is not I myself but, relative to me, a modificatum: an *other* Ego.

An actually sufficient explication of the noematic complexes involved in experience of what is alien — such an explanation as is absolutely necessary to a complete clarification of what this experience does constitutively, by constitutive association — is not yet completed with what has been shown up to now. There is need of a supplement, in order to reach the point where, on the basis of cognitions already acquired, the possibility and scope of a transcendental constitution of the Objective world can become evident and transcendental-phenomenological idealism can thus become entirely manifest.

§ 53. *Potentialities of the primordial sphere and their constitutive function in the apperception of the Other.*

As reflexively related to itself, my animate bodily organism (in my primordial sphere) [1] has the central "Here" as its mode
‹146› of givenness; every other body, / and accordingly the "other's" body, has the mode "There". This orientation, "There", can be freely changed by virtue of my kinesthesias. Thus, in my primordial sphere, the *one spatial "Nature"* is constituted throughout the change in orientations, and constituted moreover with an intentional relatedness to my animate organism as functioning perceptually. Now the fact that my bodily organism can be (and is) apprehended as a *natural body existing and movable in space like any other* is manifestly connected with the possibility expressed in the words: By free modification of my kinesthesias, particularly those of locomotion, I can change my position in such a manner that I convert any There into a Here — that is to say, I could occupy any spatial locus with my organism. This implies that, perceiving from there, I should see the same physical things, only in correspondingly different modes of appearance, such as pertain to my being there. It implies, then, that not only the systems of appearance that pertain to my current perceiving "from here", but other quite determinate systems, corresponding

---

[1] Supplied in accordance with Typescript C and the French translation.

to the change of position that puts me "there", belong constitutively to each physical thing. And the same in the case of every other "There".

Should not these interconnexions, or rather these instances of belonging together, which are involved in the primordial constitution of "my" Nature and are themselves characterized as associative — should not they be quite essential to clarification of the associative performance, experiencing someone else? After all, I do not apperceive the other ego simply as a duplicate of myself and accordingly as having my original sphere or one completely like mine. I do not apperceive him as having, more particularly, the spatial modes of appearance that are mine from here; rather, as we find on closer examination, I apperceive him as having spatial modes of appearance like those I should have if I should go over there and be where he is. Furthermore the Other is appresentatively apperceived as the "Ego" of a primordial world, and of a monad, wherein his animate organism is originally constituted and experienced in the mode of the absolute Here, precisely as the functional center for his governing. In this appresentation, therefore, the body in the mode *There*, which presents itself in *my* monadic sphere and is apperceived as another's live body (the animate organism of the alter ego) — that body indicates "the same" body in the mode *Here*, as the body experienced by the other ego in *his* monadic sphere. Moreover it indicates the "same" body concretely, with all the constitutive intentionality pertaining to this mode of givenness in the other's experience. /

§ 54. *Explicating the sense of the appresentation wherein I experience someone else.* ‹147›

Manifestly what has just now been brought to light points to the course of the association constituting the mode "Other". The body that is a member of my primordial world (the body subsequently of the other ego) is for me a body in the mode There. Its manner of appearance does not become paired in a direct association with the manner of appearance actually belonging at the time to my animate organism (in the mode Here);

rather it awakens reproductively *another*, an immediately [1]
similar appearance included in the system constitutive of my
animate organism as a body in space. It brings to mind the way
my body would look "if I were there". In this case too, although
the awakening does not become a memory *intuition*, *pairing*
takes place. The first-awakened manner of appearance of my
body is not the only thing that enters into a pairing; my body
itself does so likewise: as the synthetic unity pertaining to this
mode, and the many other familiar modes, of its appearance.
Thus the assimilative apperception becomes possible and established, by which the external body over there receives analogically from mine the sense, animate organism, and consequently the sense, organism belonging to another "world",
analogous to my primordial world.

The *general style* of this and every other apperception that
arises associatively is therefore to be described as follows: With
the associative overlapping of the data founding the apperception, there takes place an association at a higher level. If the
one datum is a particular mode of appearance of an intentional
object, which is itself an index pointing to an associatively
awakened system of manifold appearances wherein it would
show itself, then the other datum is "supplemented" to become
likewise an appearance *of* something, namely an analogous
object. But it is not as though the unity and multiplicity "thrust
upon" the latter datum merely supplemented it with modes of
appearance taken from these others. On the contrary, the analogically apprehended object and its indicated system of appearances are indeed *analogically adapted* to the analogous appearance, which has awakened this whole system too. Every
overlapping-at-a-distance, which occurs by virtue of associative
pairing, is *at the same time a fusion* and [2] therein, so far as incompatibilities do not interfere, an assimilation, an accomodation
of the sense of the one member to that of the other. /

< 148 >   If we return to our case, that of apperception of the alter ego,
it is now self-understood that what is appresented by the "body"
over there, in my primordial "surrounding world", is not

---

[1] The words "another" and "immediately" supplied in accordance with Typescript
C and the French translation.

[2] Supplied in accordance with Typescript C and the French translation.

something psychic of mine, nor anything else in my sphere of
ownness. I am *here* somatically, the center of a primordial
"world" oriented around me. Consequently my entire primordial
ownness, proper to me as a monad, has the content of the Here
— not the content varying with some "I can and do", which
might set in, and belonging to some There or other; accordingly,
not the content belonging to that definite There.[1] Each of these
contents excludes the other; they cannot both exist ‹in my
sphere of ownness› at the same time. But, since the other body
there enters into a pairing association with my body here and,
being given perceptually, becomes the core of an appresentation,
the core of my experience of a coexisting ego, that ego, according
to the whole sense-giving course of the association, must be
appresented *as an ego now coexisting in the mode There*, "such as
I should be if I were there". My own ego however, the ego given
in constant self-perception, is actual now with the content belonging to his Here. Therefore an ego is *appresented*, as *other* than
mine. That which is primordially incompatible, in simultaneous
coexistence, becomes compatible: because my primordial ego
constitutes the ego who is other for him by an appresentative
apperception, which, according to its intrinsic nature, never
demands and never is open to fulfilment by presentation.

Likewise easy to understand is the manner in which, as the
effective association goes on continuously, such an appresentation
of someone else continually furnishes new appresentational contents — that is to say, brings the changing contents of the other
ego to definite notice; and, on the other hand, the manner in
which, by virtue of the combination with a continual presentation
and the associational demands expectantly addressed to this
presentation, a *consistent confirmation* becomes possible. The
first determinate content obviously must be formed by the understanding of the other's organism and specifically organismal
conduct: the understanding of the members as hands groping
or functioning in pushing, as feet functioning in walking, as eyes
functioning in seeing, and so forth. With this the Ego at first is
determined only as governing thus somatically [*so leiblich walten-
des*] and, in a familiar manner, proves himself continually, so

---

[1] Reading with the original typescript, as given in the appendix to the published
text.

far as the whole stylistic form of the sensible processes manifest
to me primordially must correspond to the form whose type is
familiar from my own organismal governing [*leibliches Walten*].
‹149› / It is quite comprehensible that, *as a further consequence*, an
"empathizing" of definite contents belonging to the "*higher
psychic sphere*" arises. Such contents too are indicated somatically and in the conduct of the organism toward the outside world
— for example: as the outward conduct of someone who is angry
or cheerful, which I easily understand from my own conduct
under similar circumstances. Higher psychic occurrences, diverse
as they are and familiar as they have become, have furthermore
their style of synthetic interconnexions and take their course in
forms of their own, which I can understand associatively on the
basis of my empirical familiarity with the style of my own life,
as examplifying roughly differentiated typical forms. In this
sphere, moreover, every successful understanding of what occurs
in others has the effect of opening up new associations and new
possibilities of understanding; and conversely, since every pairing
association is reciprocal, every such understanding uncovers my
own psychic life in its similarity and difference and, by bringing
new features into prominence, makes it fruitful for new associations.

§ 55. *Establishment of the community of monads.*
The first form of Objectivity: intersubjective Nature.

But it is more important to clarify the *community*, developing
at various levels, which is produced forthwith by virtue of experiencing someone else: the community between me, the
primordial psychophysical Ego governing in and by means of
my primordial organism, and the appresentatively experienced
Other; then, considered more concretely and radically, between
my monadic ego and his.

The first thing constituted in the form of community, and the
foundation for all other intersubjectively common things, is the
commoness of Nature, along with that of the *Other's organism*
and *his psychophysical Ego*, as paired with *my own psychophysical
Ego*.

Since other subjectivity, by appresentation within the exclusive own-essentialness of my subjectivity, arises with the

sense and status of a subjectivity that is other in its own essence[1],
it might at first seem to be a mystery how community — even
the first community, in the form of a common world — becomes
established. The other organism, as appearing in my primordial
sphere, is first of all a body in my / primordial Nature, which is <150>
a synthetic unity belonging to me and therefore, as a determining
part included in my own essence, inseparable from me myself.
If that body functions appresentatively, then, in union with it,
the other Ego becomes an object of my consciousness — and
primarily the other Ego with his organism, as given to him in
the manner of appearance pertaining to his "absolute Here".
How can I speak at all of *the same* body, as appearing within my
primordial sphere in the mode There and within his and to him
in the mode Here? These two primordial spheres, mine which is
for me as ego the original sphere, and his which is for me an
appresented sphere — are they not *separated* by an abyss I
cannot actually cross, since crossing it would mean, after all,
that I acquired an original (rather than an appresenting) experience of someone else? If we stick to our de facto experience,
our experience of someone else as it comes to pass at any time,
we find that actually the *sensuously seen body* is experienced
forthwith as *the body of someone else* and not as merely an indi-
cation of someone else. Is not this fact an enigma?

The body belonging to my original sphere and the body
constituted, after all, quite separately in the other ego become
identified and are called the identical body of someone else. How
does this identification come about? How *can* it come about?
But the enigma appears only if the two original spheres have
already been distinguished — a distinction that already presupposes that experience of someone else has done its work. Since
we are not dealing here with a temporal genesis of such experience, on the basis of a temporally antecedent self-experience,
manifestly only a precise explication of the intentionality
actually observable in our experience of someone else and discovery of the motivations essentially implicit in that intentionality can unlock the enigma.

[1] Reading, with Typescript C, *"einer eigenwesentlich-anderen"* instead of *"einer
eigenwesentlichen anderen"* (another subjectivity having its own essence). Cf. the
French: *"ayant un être essentiellement propre"*.

As we said once before, appresentation as such presupposes a core of presentation. It is a making present combined by associations with presentation, with perception proper, but a making present that is fused with the latter in the particular function of "co-perception". In other words, the two are so fused that they stand within the *functional community of one perception*, which simultaneously presents and appresents, and yet furnishes for the total object a consciousness of its being itself there. Therefore, <151> in the object of / such a presentive-appresentive perception (an object making its appearance in the mode, itself-there), we must distinguish noematically between that part which is genuinely perceived and the rest, which is not strictly perceived and yet is indeed there too. Thus every perception of this type is transcending: it posits more as itself-there than it makes "actually" present at any time. Every external perception belongs here — for example, perception of a house (front — rear); but at bottom absolutely every perception, indeed every evidence, is thus described in respect of a most general feature, provided only that we understand "presenting" in a broader sense.

Let us apply this general cognition to the case of experiencing someone else. In this case too it should be noted that experience *can appresent only because it presents*, that here too appresentation can exist only in the aforesaid functional community with presentation. That implies, however, that, from the very beginning, *what this experience presents must belong to the unity of the very object appresented*. In other words: It is not, and cannot be, the case that the body belonging to my primordial sphere and indicating to me the other Ego (and, with him, the whole of the other primordial sphere or the other concrete ego) could appresent his factual existence and being-there-too, unless *this primordial body* acquired the sense, "a body belonging to the other ego", and, according to the whole associative-apperceptive performance, *the sense: "someone else's animate organism itself"*. Therefore it is not as though the body over there, in my primordial sphere, remained separate from the animate bodily organism of the other Ego, as if that body were something like a signal for its analogue (by virtue of an obviously inconceivable motivation); it is not as though consequently, with the spreading of the association and appresentation, my primordial Nature

and the other's appresented primordial Nature — therefore my
concrete ego and the other concrete ego — remained separate.
On the contrary, this natural body belonging to my sphere
appresents the other Ego, by virtue of the pairing association
with my bodily organism, and with my Ego governing in my
organism, within my primordially constituted Nature. In so
doing, it appresents first of all the other Ego's governing in this
body, the body over there, and mediately his governing in the
Nature that appears to him perceptually — identically the Nature
to which the body over there belongs, identically the Nature
that / is my primordial Nature. It is the same Nature, but in the <152>
mode of appearance: "as if I were standing over there, where
the Other's body is". The body is the same, given to me as the
body there, and to him as the body here, the central body.
Furthermore, "my" whole Nature is the same as the Other's.
In *my* primordial sphere it is constituted as an identical unity
of my manifold modes of givenness — an identical unity in
changing orientations around *my* animate organism (the zero
body, the body in the absolute Here), an identical unity of even
richer multiplicities that, as changing modes of appearance pertaining to different "senses", or else as changeable "perspectives",
belong to each particular orientation as here or there and also,
in a quite particular manner, belong to my animate organism,
which is inseparable from the absolute Here. All of this has for
me the originality of something included in my particular
ownness, something directly accessible in original explication of
my own self. *In the appresented other ego* the synthetic systems
are *the same*, with all their modes of appearance, accordingly
with all the possible perceptions and the noematic contents of
these: except that the *actual* perceptions and the modes of
givenness actualized therein, and also in part the objects actually
perceived, are *not the same*; rather the objects perceived are
precisely those perceivable *from there*, and *as* they are perceivable
from there. Something similar is true of anything else of my own
and the corresponding alien thing, even where original explication does not go on in perceptions. I do not have an appresented
second original sphere with a second "Nature" and, in this Nature,
a second animate bodily organism (the one belonging to the
other ego himself), so that I must then ask how I can apprehend

my Nature and this other as modes of appearance of the same
Objective Nature. On the contrary, the *identity*-sense of "my"
primordial Nature and the presentiated other primordial Nature
is *necessarily* produced by the appresentation and the unity
that it, *as* appresentation, necessarily has with the presentation
co-functioning for it — this appresentation by virtue of which
an Other and, consequently, his concrete ego are there for me
in the first place. Quite rightly, therefore, we speak of *perceiving*
someone else and then of perceiving the Objective world, perceiving that the other Ego and I are looking at the same world,
and so forth — though this perceiving goes on exclusively within
the sphere of my ownness. That does not at all contravene the
fact that the intentionality of this sphere transcends my owness,
‹153› or the fact that accordingly my ego / constitutes in himself
another ego — and constitutes this ego, moreover, as existent.
What I actually see is not a sign and not a mere analogue, a
depiction in any natural sense of the word; on the contrary, it
is someone else. And what is grasped with actual originariness
in this seeing — namely that corporeality over there, or rather
only one aspect of its surface — is the Other's body itself, but
seen just from my position and in respect of this aspect: According to the sense-constitution involved in perceiving someone
else, what is grasped originaliter is the body of a psyche essentially inaccessible to me originaliter, and the two are comprised in the unity of one psychophysical reality.

On the other hand, it is implicit in the intentional essence of
this perception of the Other — the Other who exists henceforth,
as I do myself, within what is henceforth the Objective world —
that I as perceiver can find the aforesaid distinction between my
primordial sphere and the merely presentiated primordial sphere
of the Other, and consequently can trace the peculiarities of the
division into two noetic strata and explicate the complexes of
associative intentionality. The experiential phenomenon, Objective Nature, has, besides the primordially constituted stratum,
a superimposed second, merely appresented stratum originating
from my experiencing of someone else; and this fact concerns,
first of all, *the Other's animate bodily organism*, which is, so to
speak, *the intrinsically first Object*, just as *the other man is constitutionally the intrinsically first ‹Objective› man*. In the case of

this primal phenomenon of Objectivity, the situation is already clear to us: If I screen off my experience of someone else, I have the lowest constitution, the one-layered presentive constitution of the other body within my primordial sphere; if I add that experience, I have appresentationally, and as coinciding synthetically with the presentational stratum, the same animate organism as it is given to the other Ego himself, and I have the further possible modes of givenness available to him.

From that, as is easily understandable, *every* natural Object experienced or experienceable by me in the lower stratum receives an appresentational stratum (though by no means one that becomes explicitly intuited), a stratum united in an identifying synthesis with the stratum given to me in the mode of primordial originality: the same natural Object in its possible modes of givenness to the other Ego. This is repeated, *mutatis mutandis*, in the case of subsequently constituted mundanities of the concrete Objective world as it always exists for us: namely as a world of men and culture. /

The following should be noted in this connexion. It is implicit <154> in the sense of my successful apperception of others that their world, the world belonging to their appearance-systems, must be experienced forthwith as the same as the world belonging to my appearance-systems; and this involves an identity of our appearance-systems. Now we know very well that there are such things as *"abnormalities"* (for example: in the case of subjects who are blind or deaf); we know that therefore the appearance-systems are by no means always absolutely identical and that whole strata (though not all strata) can differ. But abnormality must first be *constituted* as such; and the constituting of abnormality is possible only on the basis of an intrinsically antecedent normality. This points to new tasks, which belong to a higher level of phenomenological analysis of the constitutional origin of the Objective world — as the Objective world existing for us and only by virtue of our own sense-producing sources, a world that can have neither sense nor existence for us otherwise. The Objective world has existence by virtue of a harmonious confirmation of the apperceptive constitution, once this has succeeded: a confirmation thereof by the continuance of experiencing life with a consistent harmoniousness, which always becomes re-established as extending through any "corrections" that may be required to that end. Now harmoniousness is preserved also by virtue of a recasting of apperceptions through distinguishing between normality and abnormalities (as modifications thereof), or by virtue of the constitution of new unities throughout the changes involved in abnormalities. Among the problems of abnormality the problem of non-human animality and that of the levels of "higher and lower" brutes are included. Relative to the brute, man is, constitutionally speaking, the normal case — just as I myself am the primal norm constitutionally for all other men. Brutes are essentially constituted for me as abnormal "variants" of my humanness, even though *among* them in turn normality and abnormality may be differentiated. Always it is a matter of intentional modifications in the sense-structure itself, as what becomes evinced. All of that, to be sure, needs a more thorough phenomenological explication. This general account, however, is enough for our present purposes.

After these clarifications it is no longer an enigma how I can constitute in myself another Ego or, more radically, how I can constitute in my monad another monad, and can experience what is constituted in me as nevertheless other than me. At the same time, this being indeed inseparable from such constitution, ‹155› it is no longer an enigma how I / can identify a Nature constituted in me with a Nature constituted by someone else (or, stated with the necessary precision, how I can identify a Nature constituted in me with one constituted in me *as* a Nature constituted by someone else). This identification is no greater enigma than any other synthetic identification. It is therefore no more mysterious than any, by virtue of which, as an identification confined to my own original sphere, no matter what objective unity acquires sense and being for me through the medium of *presentiations*. Let us consider the following instructive example and use it to bring out a thought that takes us further: the notion of a *connexion* constituted through the medium of presentiation. How does one of my own subjective processes acquire for me the sense and status of an existent process, something existing with its identical temporal form and identical temporal content? The original is gone; but, in repeated presentiations,

I go back to it and do so with the evidence: "I can always do so again." But these repeated presentations are evidently themselves a temporal sequence; and each is separate from the others. In spite of that, however, an identifying synthesis connects them in the evident consciousness of "the Same" — which implies the same, never repeated temporal form, filled with the same content. Here, as everywhere else, "the Same" signifies therefore an *identical intentional object of separate conscious processes,* hence an object immanent in them only as something *non-really* inherent. Another case, very important in itself, is that of the constitution of objects that are ideal in the pregnant sense — for example: all logically ideal objects. In a living, many-membered thinking action I produce a structure: a theorem or a numerical structure. Subsequently I repeat the producing, while recollecting my earlier producing. At once, and by essential necessity, an identifying synthesis takes place; furthermore a new identifying synthesis occurs with each additional repetition (a repetition performed with a consciousness that the producing can be repeated again at will): It is identically the same proposition, identically the same numerical structure, *but repeatedly produced* or, this being equivalent, repeatedly made evident. Therefore in this case, through the medium of recollective presentations, the synthesis extends — within my stream of subjective processes (which always is already constituted) — from my living present into my currently relevant separate pasts and thus makes a *connexion* between my present and these pasts. With that, moreover, the supremely significant *transcendental problem of ideal objectivities* ("ideal" in the specific sense) is solved. Their supertemporality turns out to be *omnitemporality,* as a correlate of free / produceability and ‹156› reproduceability at all times. After constitution of the Objective world with its Objective time and its Objective men as possible thinking subjects, that obviously carries over to ideal structures, as themselves Objectivated, and to their Objective omnitemporality. Thus the contrast between them and Objective *realities,* as spatiotemporally individuated structures, becomes understandable.

If we return now to our case, the experience of someone else, we find that, with its complicated structure, it effects a similar

connexion mediated by presentiation: namely a connexion between, on the one hand, the uninterruptedly living self-experience (as purely passive original self-appearance) of the concrete
ego — accordingly, his primordial sphere — and, on the other
hand, the *alien sphere* presentiated therein. It effects this, first,
by its identifying synthesis of the *primordially given* animate
body of someone else and the same animate body, but *appresented* in other modes of appearance, and secondly, spreading
out from there, by its identifying synthesis of the same Nature,
given and verified primordially (with pure sensuous originality)
and at the same time appresentationally. In that way the
coexistence of my <polar> Ego and the other Ego, of my whole
concrete ego and his, my intentional life and his, my "realities"
and his — in short, a *common time-form* — is primally instituted;
and thus every primordial temporality automatically acquires
the significance of being merely an original mode of appearance
of Objective temporality to a particular subject. In this connexion we see that the temporal community of the constitutively interrelated monads is indissoluble, because it is tied
up essentially with the constitution of *a world and a world time.*

§ 56. *Constitution of higher levels of intermonadic community.*

With these considerations we have clarified the *first and lowest
level of communalization* between me, the primordial monad for
myself, and the monad constituted in me, yet as other and
accordingly as existing for himself but only appresentationally
demonstrable to me. The only conceivable manner in which
others can have for me the sense and status of existent others,
thus and so determined, consists in their being constituted *in me*
as others. If they get that sense and status from sources that
yield a continual confirmation, then they do indeed *exist* (as I /
<157> am *compelled* to say), but exclusively as having the sense with
which they are constituted: as monads, existing for themselves
precisely as I exist for myself, yet existing also in communion,
therefore (I emphasize the expression already used earlier) in
connexion with me qua concrete ego, qua monad. To be sure, they
are separate from my monad, so far as really inherent constituents are concerned, since no really inherent connexion leads

from their subjective processes to my subjective processes or from anything included in their peculiar ownness to anything included in mine. To that separation there corresponds, after all, the *"real"*, the mundane separation of my psychophysical existence from someone else's, a separation that shows itself as spatial, owing to the spatial character of our Objective animate organisms. On the other hand, this original communion is not just nothing. Whereas, really inherently, each monad is an absolutely separate unity, the "irreal" intentional reaching of the other into my primordiality is not irreal in the sense of being dreamt into it or being present to consciousness after the fashion of a mere phantasy. *Something that exists is in intentional communion with something else that exists.* It is an essentially *unique connectedness*, an actual community and precisely the one that makes transcendentally possible the being of a world, a world of men and things.

After the first level of communalization and (this being almost equivalent) the first constitution of an Objective world, starting from the primordial world, have been sufficiently clarified, the *higher levels* offer relatively minor difficulties. Though comprehensive investigations and a progressive differentiation of problems relating to these levels are necessary for purposes of an all-round explication, here we can be satisfied with rough general indications, easily understandable on the basis already laid. Starting from me, from the one who is constitutionally the primal monad, I acquire what are for me other monads and, correlatively, others as *psychophysical* subjects. This implies that I do *not* acquire the latter *merely as over against me* somatically and — by virtue of associative pairing — as *related back to my psychophysical existence* (which indeed is universally "central", and particularly the "central member" in the communalized world of the present level because of the necessarily oriented manner in which this world is given). On the contrary (and this carries over to the sociality of brute animals), in the sense of *a community of men* and in that of *man* — who, even as solitary, has the sense: member of a community — there is implicit a *mutual being for one another*, which / entails an *Objectivating equalization* ‹158› of my existence with that of all others — consequently: I or anyone else, as a man among other men. If, with my understanding of someone else, I penetrate more deeply into him, into his horizon of ownness, I shall soon run into the fact that, just as his animate bodily organism lies in my field of perception, so my animate organism lies in his field of perception and that, in general, he experiences me forthwith as an Other for him, just as I experience him as *my* Other. Likewise I shall find that, in the case of a plurality of Others, they are experienced also by one another as Others, and consequently that I can experience any given Other not only as himself an Other but also as related in turn to *his* Others and perhaps — with a mediatedness that may be conceived as reiterable — related at the same time to me. It is also clear that men become apperceivable only as finding Others and still more Others, not just in the realm of actuality but likewise in the realm of possibility, at their own pleasure. Openly endless Nature itself then becomes a Nature that includes an open plurality of men (conceived more generally: animalia), distributed one knows not how in infinite space, as subjects of possible intercommunion. To this community there naturally corresponds, in transcendental concreteness, a similarly [1] open *community of monads*, which we designate as *transcendental intersubjectivity*. We need hardly say that, as existing for me,[2] it is constituted purely within me, the meditating ego, purely by virtue of sources belonging to my intentionality; nevertheless it is constituted thus *as* a community constituted also in every other monad (who, in turn, is constituted with the modification: "other") as the same community — only with a different subjective mode of appearance — and as necessarily bearing within itself the same Objective world. Manifestly it is essentially necessary to the world constituted transcendentally in me (and similarly necessary to the world constituted in any community of monads that is imaginable by me) that it be a *world of men* and that, *in each particular man*, it be more or less perfectly constituted *intrapsychically* — in intentional processes and potential systems of intentionality, which, as "psychic life", are themselves already constituted as existing in the world. By "the psychic constitution of the

---

[1] Reading *"entsprechend"* instead of *"entsprechende"* (similar), as in both the published text and Typescript C.

[2] Reading with Typescript C and the French version. According to the published text: "that for me".

Objective world" we mean, for example, my actual and possible experience of the world, as an experience belonging to me, the Ego who experiences himself as a man. Such experience of the world is more or less perfect; it always has its [1] open undetermined horizon. For each man, every other is implicit in this horizon — physically, / psychophysically, in respect of what is <159> internal to the other's psyche — and is thus in principle a realm of endless accessibilities, though in fact most other men remain horizonal.

§ 57. *Clarification of the parallel between explication of what is internal to the psyche and egological transcendental explication.*

On this basis it is not hard to clear up the *necessary parallel between explications of what is internal to the psyche and egological transcendental explications,* or the fact that, as was already said earlier, the pure psyche is a *self-Objectivation* of the monad, accomplished in the latter — a self-Objectivation the different levels of which are essential necessities, if Others are possibly to exist for the monad.

Connected with this is the fact that, a priori, every analysis or theory of transcendental phenomenology — including the theory whose main features have just been indicated, the theory of transcendental constitution of an Objective world — can be produced in the natural realm, when we give up the transcendental attitude. Thus transposed to the realm of transcendental naïveté, it becomes a theory pertaining to internal psychology. *Whether the two disciplines be eidetic or empirical,* a *"pure" psychology* — a psychology that merely explicates what belongs to a psyche, to a concrete human Ego, as its own intentional essence — corresponds to a *transcendental phenomenology,* and vice versa. That, however, is something to be made evident transcendentally.

§ 58. *Differentiation of problems in the intentional analysis of higher intersubjective communities. I and my surrounding world.*

The *constitution of humanity,* or of that community which belongs to the full essence of humanity, does not end with what

[1] Reading with Typescript C, "*sie hat stets ihren*", instead of "*aber doch mindestens als*". Cf. the French: "*elle a toujours ses*".

has been considered up to now. On the basis, however, of community in the last sense acquired, it is easy to understand [1] the possibility of *acts of the Ego that reach into the other Ego through the medium of appresentative experience of someone else* and, indeed, the possibility of *specifically personal acts of the Ego* that have the character of acts of mine directed to you [2], the character of *social acts*, by means of which all human personal communication is established. To study these acts carefully in their different forms and, starting from there, to make the essence of all *sociality* transcendentally understandable is an ‹160› important task. With / communalization proper, *social communalization*, there become constituted within the Objective world, as spiritual Objectivities of a peculiar kind, the various types of social communities with their possible hierarchical order —, among them the pre-eminent types that have the character of *"personalities of a higher order"*.

Consequently there would come into consideration, as inseparable from and (in a certain sense) correlative to the set of problems indicated, the problem of the constitution of the specifically human surrounding world, a surrounding world of culture for each man and each human community; likewise the problem of the genuine, though restricted, kind of Objectivity belonging to such a world. Its Objectivity is restricted, though concretely the world is given to me and to everyone only as a cultural world and as having the sense: accessible to everyone. But, as soon becomes apparent when its sense is explicated precisely, there are essential constitutional reasons why this accessibility is not unconditional. In this respect it is manifestly different from that absolutely unconditional accessibility to everyone which belongs essentially to the constitutional sense of Nature, of the animate organism, and therefore of the psychophysical man (understood with a certain generality). To be sure, the following is also included in the sphere of unconditional universality which is the correlate of the essential form

---

[1] Reading with Typescript C: *"Aber verständlich ist sehr leicht"*, instead of *"Aber selbstverständlich ist es sehr leicht"* (But of course it is very easy), which makes the sentence incomplete. Cf. the French: *"on comprend facilement"*.

[2] The phrase, "the character of acts of mine directed to you", supplied in accordance with Typescript C, *"von Ich-Du-Akten"*, and the French, *"d'actes allant 'de moi a toi' "*.

of world constitution: Everyone, as a matter of apriori necessity, lives in the same Nature, a Nature moreover that, with the necessary communalization of his life and the lives of others, he has fashioned into a *cultural world* in his individual and communalized living and doing — a world having human significances, even if it belongs to an extremely low cultural level. But this, after all, does not exclude, either a priori or de facto, the truth that men belonging to one and the same world live in a loose cultural community — or even none at all — and accordingly constitute different surrounding worlds of culture, as concrete life-worlds in which the relatively or absolutely separate communities live their passive and active lives. Each man understands first of all, in respect of a core and as having its unrevealed horizon, *his* concrete surrounding world or *his* culture; and he does so precisely as a man who belongs to the community fashioning it historically. A deeper understanding, one that opens up the horizon of the past (which is co-determinant for an understanding of the present itself), is essentially possible to all members of that community, with a certain originality possible to them alone / and barred to anyone from <161> another community who enters into relation with theirs. At first such an individual necessarily understands men of the alien world as generically men, and men of a "certain" cultural world. Starting from there, he must first produce for himself, step by step, the possibilities of further understanding. Starting from what is most generally understandable, he must first open up ways of access to a sympathetic understanding of broader and broader strata of the present and then of the historical past, which in turn helps him to gain broader access to the present.

Constitution of "worlds" of any kind whatever, beginning with one's own stream of subjective processes, with its openly endless multiplicities, and continuing up through the Objective world with its various levels of Objectivation, is subject to the law of *"oriented" constitution*,[1] a constitution that presupposes at various levels, but within the extension of a sense conceived with maximal breadth, something "primordially" and something

---

[1] In accordance with Typescript C and the French translation, the passage of the published text that follows here, p. 161, 11. 15–21, is assigned a later position. See the next note.

"secondarily" constituted. At each of the levels in question, the primordial enters, with a new stratum of sense, into the secondarily constituted world; and this occurs in such a fashion that the primordial becomes the central member, in accordance with orientational modes of givenness. The secondarily constituted, as a "world", is necessarily given as a horizon of being that is accessible from the primordial and is discoverable in a particular order. It is already thus in the case of the first, the "immanent" world, which we call the stream of subjective processes. As a system of mutual externalities, this stream is given in an orientation around the primordially constituted living present, from which everything else outside it (but belonging to immanent temporality) is accessible. Again, within the sphere that is primordial in our specific sense, my animate organism is the central member of "Nature", the "world" that becomes constituted by means of governance of my organism. In like manner, my psychophysical organism is primordial for the constitution of the Objective world of mutual externalities, and, in accordance with the oriented mode of givenness of this world, enters it as the central member. If the "world" that is primordial in our
‹162› distinctive sense / does not itself become the center of the Objective world, the reason is that this whole primordial "world" becomes Objectivated in such a fashion that it produces no new mutual externalities. On the other hand, the multiplicity of the Other's world is given as oriented peripherally to mine, and is thus a world, because it becomes constituted with a common Objective world immanent in it, and the spatiotemporal form of this Objective world functions at the same time as a form that gives access to it.

   If we return to our case, that of the cultural world, we find that it too, as a world of cultures, is given orientedly on the underlying basis of the Nature common to all and on the basis of the spatiotemporal form that gives access to Nature and must function also in making the multiplicity of cultural formations
‹161› and cultures accessible. / We see that in this fashion the cultural world too is given "orientedly", in relation to a zero member or a ‹zero› "personality". Here I and my culture are primordial, over against every alien culture. To me and to those who share in my culture, an alien culture is accessible only by a kind of

"experience of someone else", a kind of "empathy", by which we project ourselves into the alien cultural community and its culture. This empathy also calls for intentional investigations.[1] /

We must forgo a more precise exploration of the sense-stratum ‹ 162 › that gives to the world of humanity and culture, as such, its specific sense. thus making it a world endowed with specifically "spiritual" predicates. Our constitutional explications have shown the intentional motivational complexes wherein accrued that coherent substratum of the full concrete world which is left us if we abstract from all predicates belonging to "Objective spirit". We retain the whole of Nature, already constituted as a concrete unity in itself. We retain, as included in Nature, the animate organisms of men and brutes; but we no longer retain psychic life as concretely complete, since human existence as such is always related consciously to an existent practical world as a surrounding world already endowed with humanly significant predicates, and this relationship presupposes a psychological constitution of such predicates.

That every such predicate of the world accrues from a *temporal* genesis and, indeed, one that is rooted in human undergoing and doing, needs no proof. A presupposition for the origin of such predicates in the particular subjects (and for the origin of their intersubjective acceptance as abiding predicates of the common life-world) is, consequently, that a community of men and each particular man are vitally immersed in a concrete surrounding world, are related to it in undergoing and doing — that all of this is already constituted. With this continual change in the human life-world, manifestly *the men themselves also change as persons*, since correlatively they must always be taking on new habitual properties. In this connexion / far-reaching problems ‹163› of static and genetic constitution make themselves keenly felt, those of genetic constitution as part of the problem of all-embracing genesis, which presents so many enigmas. For example: regarding personality, not only the problem of the static constitution of a unity of personal character, over against the multiplicity of instituted and subsequently annulled habitualities,

---

[1] In accordance with Typescript C and the French translation, the passage beginning "We see . . ." has been transposed. See the preceding note.

but also the *genetic* problem, which leads back to enigmas concerning *"innate" character.*

For the present it must suffice that we have indicated these problems of a higher level as problems of constitution and thereby made it understandable that, with the systematic progress of transcendental-phenomenological explication of the apodictic ego, the transcendental sense of the world must also become disclosed to us ultimately in the *full concreteness* with which it is incessantly the *life-world* for us all. That applies likewise to all the particular formations of the surrounding world, wherein it presents itself to us according to our personal upbringing and development or according to our membership in this or that nation, this or that cultural community. All these matters are governed by essential necessities; they conform to an essential style, which derives its necessity from the transcendental ego and then from the transcendental intersubjectivity which discloses itself in that ego — accordingly, from the essential forms of transcendental motivation and transcendental constitution. If we succeed in uncovering these forms, the aforesaid apriori style acquires a rational clarification that has the highest dignity, the dignity of an ultimate, a transcendental intelligibility.

§ 59. *Ontological explication and its place within constitutional transcendental phenomenology as a whole.*

By our coherent bits of actually executing analysis and, in part, by the accompanying predelineation of inevitable new problems and the form of order they demand, we have acquired philosophically fundamental insights. Starting from the experiential world given beforehand as existent and (with the shift to the eidetic attitude) from any experiential world whatever, conceived as given beforehand as existent, we exercised transcendental reduction — that is: we went back to the / transcendental ego, who constitutes within himself givenness-beforehand and all modes of subsequent givenness; or (with eidetic self-variation) we went back to any transcendental ego whatever.

The transcendental ego was conceived accordingly as an ego who experiences within himself a world, who proves a world

‹164›

harmoniously. Tracing the essence of such constitution and its egological levels, we made visible an Apriori of a completely [1] novel kind, namely the Apriori of constitution. We learned to distinguish, on the one hand, the self-constitution of the ego for himself and in his primordial own-essentialness and, on the other hand, the constitution of all the aliennesses of various levels, by virtue of sources belonging to his own essentialness. There resulted the all-embracing unity of the essential form belonging to the total constitution accomplished in my own ego — the constitution as whose correlate the Objectively existing world, for me and for any ego whatever, is continually given beforehand, and goes on being shaped in its sense-strata, with a [2] correlative apriori form-style. And this constitution is itself an Apriori. With this most radical and consequential explication of what is intentionally included and what becomes intentionally motivated in "my" ego and in my essential variants, it becomes apparent that the universal de facto structure of the given Objective world — as mere Nature, as psychophysical being, as humanness, sociality of various levels, and culture — is, to a very great extent (and perhaps much further than we yet can see), an *essential necessity*. An understandable and necessary consequence is that the *task of an apriori ontology of the real world* — which is precisely discovery of the Apriori belonging to this world's universality — is inevitable but, on the other hand, one-sided and not philosophical in the final sense. Such an ontological Apriori (for example: of Nature, of the psychophysical, of sociality and culture) does indeed confer on the ontic fact, on the de facto world in respect of its "accidental" features, a relative intelligibility, that of an evident necessity of being thus and so by virtue of eidetic laws; but it does not confer *philosophical* — that is, *transcendental*, intelligibility. Philosophy, after all, demands an elucidation by virtue of the *ultimate* and *most concrete* essential necessities; and these are the necessities that satisfy the essential rootedness of any Objective world in transcendental subjectivity and thus make the world intelligible concretely: *as a constituted sense.* Only then, moreover, / do the ‹165›

---

[1] Supplied in accordance with Typescript C and the French translation.
[2] Reading "*einem*" instead of "*meinem*" (my), as in both the published text and Typescript C. Cf. the French translation: "*une forme*".

"supreme and final" questions become disclosed, those that are still to be addressed to the world even as understood in this manner.

One consequence of the beginning phase of phenomenology was that its method of pure but at the same time eidetic intuition led to attempts at a new ontology, fundamentally different in essence from the ontology of the eighteenth century, which operated logically with concepts remote from intuition; or, this being the same thing, attempts to draw *directly from concrete intuition*, in order to build particular apriori sciences (pure grammar, pure logic, pure jurisprudence, the eidetic theory of intuitively experienced Nature, and so forth) and, embracing them all, a universal ontology of the Objective world. As regards this, nothing prevents starting at first quite concretely with the human life-world around us, and with man himself as essentially related to this our surrounding world, and exploring, indeed purely intuitively, the extremely copious and never-discovered Apriori of any such surrounding world whatever, taking this Apriori as the point of departure for a systematic explication of human existence and of world strata that disclose themselves correlatively in the latter. But what is acquired there straightforwardiy, though it is a system of the Apriori, becomes philosophically intelligible and (according to what was said just now) an Apriori related back to the ultimate sources of understanding, only when problems of constitution, as problems of the specifically philosophical level, become disclosed and the natural realm of knowledge is at the same time exchanged for the transcendental. This implies that everything natural, everything given beforehand in straightforward intuition, must be built up again with a new originariness and not interpreted merely sequaciously as already definitive. That a procedure drawing insight from eidetic intuition is called phenomenological and claims philosophical significance is justified only by the circumstance that every genuine intuition has its place in the constitutional nexus. For this reason every intuitive ascertainment, in the attitude of positivity, concerning the sphere of eidetically necessary (axiomatic) fundamentals serves as *preliminary work* and is even indispensible a priori. It furnishes [1]

---

[1] Reading with Typescript C and the French translation. According to the published text: "Its result must become ...".

the transcendental clue for discovery of the full constitutive concretion, as having both a noetic and a noematic aspect.

Regardless of the fact that it / uncovers hidden horizons of ‹166› sense on the ontic side (the overlooking of which seriously restricts the value of apriori ascertainments and makes their application uncertain), the significance and complete novelty of this going back into the constitutive is shown by the "monadological" results of our investigation.

§ 60. *Metaphysical results of our explication of experiencing someone else.*

Our monadological results are *metaphysical*, if it be true that ultimate cognitions of being should be called metaphysical. On the other hand, what we have here is *anything but metaphysics in the customary sense:* a historically degenerate metaphysics, which by no means conforms to the sense with which metaphysics, as "first philosophy", was instituted originally. Phenomenology's purely intuitive, concrete, and also apodictic mode of demonstration excludes all "metaphysical adventure", all speculative excesses.

Let us bring into relief some of *our* metaphysical results and at the same time draw further consequences.

A priori, my ego, given to me apodictically — the only thing I can posit in absolute apodicticity as existing — can be a world-experiencing ego only by being in communion with others like himself: a member of a community of monads, which is given orientedly, starting from himself. In that the Objective world of experience shows itself consistently, other monads show themselves consistently to be existent. Conversely, I cannot conceive a plurality of monads otherwise than as explicitly or implicitly in communion. This involves being a plurality of monads that constitutes in itself an Objective world and that spatializes, temporalizes, realizes itself — psychophysically and, in particular, as human beings — within that world. It is essentially necessary that the *togetherness* of monads, their mere *co*-existence, be a *temporal* co-existence and then also an existence temporalized in the form: *"real"* temporality.

But that entails further extremely important metaphysical

results. Is it conceivable (to me, the subject who asks this, or, starting from me, any conceivable subject who might ask it) — is it, I ask, *conceivable* that two or more *separate pluralities of monads*, i.e. pluralities *not in communion*, co-exist, each of which accordingly constitutes *a world of its own*, so that together they ‹167› constitute *two* / worlds that are separate ad infinitum, *two* infinite *spaces and space-times*? Manifestly, instead of being a conceivability, that is a pure absurdity. A priori, as the *unity* of an intersubjectivity (an intersubjectivity, moreover, that possibly lacks every actual relation of community with the other intersubjectivity), each of two such groups of monads has, to be sure, its possibly quite different looking "world". But the two worlds are then necessarily *mere "surrounding worlds"*, belonging to these two intersubjectivities respectively, and mere aspects of a single Objective world, which is *common* to them. For indeed the two intersubjectivities are not absolutely isolated. As imagined by me, each of them is in necessary communion with me (or with me in respect of a possible variant of myself) as the constitutive primal monad relative to them. Accordingly they belong in truth to a single universal community, which includes me and comprises unitarily all the monads and groups of monads that can be conceived as co-existent. Actually, therefore, *there can exist only a single community of monads*, the community of *all* co-existing monads. Hence there can exist *only one Objective world*, only one Objective time, only one Objective space, only one Objective Nature. Moreover this one Nature *must* exist, if there are any structures in me that involve the co-existence of other monads. This alone is possible: that different groups of monads and different worlds are related to one another as those that may belong to stellar worlds we cannot see are related to us — that is, with animalia who lack all *actual* connexion with us. Their worlds, however, are surrounding worlds with open horizons that are only de facto, only accidentally, undiscoverable to them.

But the sense of this uniqueness of both the monadological world and the Objective world "innate" in it must be correctly understood. Naturally Leibniz is right when he says that infinitely many monads and groups of monads are conceivable but that it does not follow that all these possibilities are *com-*

possible; and, again, when he says that infinitely many worlds might have been "created", but not two or more at once, since they are imcompossible. It is to be noted in this connexion that, in a free variation, I can phantasy *first of all myself*, this apodictic de facto ego, as otherwise and can thus acquire the *system of possible variants of myself*, each of which, however, is annuled by each of the others and by the ego who I actually am. It is *a system of apriori | incompossibility*. Furthermore the fact, "I ‹168› am", prescribes *whether* other monads are others for me and *what* they are for me. I can only find them; I cannot create others that shall exist for me. If I phantasy myself as a pure possibility different from what I actually am, that possibility in turn prescribes what monads exist for him as others. And, proceeding in this fashion, I recognize that *each monad having the status of a concrete possibility predelineates a compossible universe*, a closed "world of monads", and that two worlds of monads are incompossible, just as two possible variants of my ego (or of any presupposedly phantasied ego whatever) are incompossible.

Such results and the course of the investigations leading to them enable us to understand how questions that, for traditional philosophy, had to lie beyond all the limits of science can acquire sense (regardless of how they may be decided) — for example, problems we touched on earlier.

§ 61. *The traditional problems of "psychological origins" and their phenomenological clarification.*

Within the world of men and brutes, we encounter the familiar natural-scientific problems of psychophysical, physiological, and psychological genesis. Among them is included the problem of psychic genesis. It is suggested to us by the development, in the course of which every child must build up his "idea of the world". The apperceptive system in which a world, as a realm of actual and possible experience, is there for him and always given beforehand must first of all become constituted in the course of the child's psychic development. The child, considered Objectively, comes "into the world". How does he come to a "beginning" of his psychic life?

This psychophysical coming into the world leads back to the problem of live-bodily (purely "biological") individual development and phylogenesis, which, for its part, has its parallel in a psychological phylogenesis. But does that not point to corresponding interconnexions among the transcendental absolute monads, since indeed, so far as their psyches are concerned, men and brutes are self-Objectivations of monads? Should not this whole situation indicate most serious essential problems for a constitutional phenomenology, as "transcendental philosophy"?/

<169>   To a great extent genetic problems, and naturally those of the first and most fundamental level, have indeed already been dealt with in the actual work of phenomenology. The fundamental level is, of course, the one pertaining to "my" ego in respect of his primordial own-essentialness. Constitution on the part of the consciousness of internal time and the whole phenomenological theory of association belong here; and what my primordial ego finds in original intuitive self-explication applies to every other ego forthwith, and for essential reasons. But with that, to be sure, the above-indicated *genetic problems of birth and death and the generative nexus of psychophysical being* have not yet been touched. Manifestly they belong to a higher dimension and presuppose such a tremendous labor of explication pertaining to the lower spheres that it will be a long time before they can become problems to work on.

Within the working sphere, however, let us indicate more precisely certain vast domains of problems (both static and genetic) that bring us into a closer relation to the philosophical tradition. Our connected intentional clarifications of the experience of someone else and the constitution of an Objective world took place on a basis given us beforehand in the transcendental attitude: a structural articulation of the primordial sphere, in which we already found a world, a primordial one. It had become accessible to us starting from the concrete world, taken qua "phenomenon", by means of that peculiar primordial reduction of the latter to what belongs to my ownness: a "world" of immanent transcendencies. It included the whole of Nature, reduced to the Nature appertaining to me myself by virtue of *my* pure sensuousness; but it included likewise the psychophysical man (with his psyche) as correspondingly reduced. As regards

"Nature", not only "sight things", "touch things", and the like, but also to some extent complete physical things as substrates of causal properties were included, along with the all-embracing forms: space and time. Obviously the *first* problem for the constitutional clarification of the existential sense of the Objective world is to clarify the *origin of this primordial "Nature"* and that of the *primordial unity* [1] *of animate organism and psyche* — to clarify the constituting of them / as immanent ‹170› transcendencies. Actually to do so requires extraordinarily extensive investigations.

In this connexion we are again reminded of the problems concerning the "psychological origin" of the "idea of space", the "idea of time", the "idea of a physical thing" — problems dealt with so often in the last century by the most distinguished physiologists and psychologists. Much as the great projects bore the stamp of their distinguished authors, no actual clarification has as yet been attained.

When we turn from them to the set of problems that we have delimited and fitted into the phenomenological system of levels, it is evident that the whole of modern psychology and epistemology has failed to grasp the *proper sense* of the problems to be set here, both *psychologically and transcendentally* — their sense, namely, as problems of (static and genetic) *intentional explication.* To grasp it was, after all, impossible even for those who had accepted Brentano's doctrine of "psychic phenomena" as intentional processes. There was a lack of understanding for the peculiar character of an intentional "analysis" and all the tasks disclosed by consciousness as such, in respect of noesis and noema, a lack of understanding for the fundamentally novel methods these tasks require. About problems that concern the "psychological origins of the ideas of space, time, and the physical thing" no physics or physiology and no experimental or non-experimental psychology that moves similarly in the realm of inductive externalities has anything to say. Those are quite exclusively problems of intentional constitution that concern phenomena which are already given us beforehand as "clues" (or perhaps can become given beforehand, in particular, with

---

[1] Reading ,,*Einheit*'' instead of ''*Einheiten*'' (unities) as in both the published text and Typescript C. In the French translation: "*unités*".

the aid of an experiment), but which must now be interrogated for the first time according to the intentional method and *within the universal complexes of psychic constitution*. The kind of universality meant here is shown with sufficient distinctness in the case of the systematic unitary complex of those constitutions that are explicata of my ego, in respect of what is peculiar to my own self and what is other.

Phenomenology signifies indeed a fundamental refashioning of psychology too. Accordingly, by far the greater part of psychological research belongs in an *apriori and pure intentional psychology*. (Here the word "pure" means: kept free from everything psychophysical.) It is the same psychology, concerning which we ‹171› have already/indicated repeatedly that, by means of a change of the natural into the transcendental attitude, it is open to a "Copernican conversion", wherewith it assumes the new sense of a completely radical transcendental consideration of the world and impresses this sense on all phenomenological-psychological analyses. This sense alone makes such a psychology utilizable for transcendental philosophy and, indeed, gives it a place within a transcendental "metaphysics". Precisely in this lies the ultimate clarification and overcoming of the *transcendental psychologism* that has misled and paralysed the whole of modern philosophy.

As in the case of transcendental phenomenology, so also in the parallel case of intentional psychology (as a "positive" science) our exposition has manifestly predelineated a *fundamental structure*, a division of the corresponding investigations of eidetic psychology into those that explicate intentionally what is included in the *concrete own-essentiality of any psyche whatever* and those that explicate the intentionality pertaining to the otherness that becomes constituted therein. To the former sphere of research belongs the chief and fundamental part of the intentional explication of one's "idea of the world" — stated more precisely, explication of the "phenomenon", which makes its appearance within the human psyche: the existing world, as the world of universal experience. If this experiential world is reduced to the world constituted primordially in the single psyche, it is no longer everyone's world, the world that gets its sense from communalized human experience, but is exclusively this intentional correlate of the experiencing life that goes on in a single psyche, and first of all my experiencing life and its sense-fashionings in primordial originariness at various levels. Tracing these fashionings, intentional explication has to make consti-tutionally understandable this primordial core of the phenome-nal world — this core, which every one of us men and, above all, every psychologist can acquire by the already-described exclusion of sense-moments pertaining to "otherness". If, within this primordial "world", we abstract from the reduced psychophysical being, "I, the man", primordial bare Nature remains, as the Nature pertaining to my own "bare sensuousness". As an initial problem concerning the psychological origin of the experiential world, there emerges here the problem concerning the origin of the "thing-phantom", or "thing pertaining to the senses", with its strata (sight thing, ‹touch thing,› and so forth) and their synthetic unity. The thing-phantom is / given (always ‹172› within the limits set by this primordial reduction) purely as a unity belonging to modes of sensuous appearance and their syntheses. The thing-phantom, in its variants as "near thing" and "far thing", all of which belong together synthetically, is not yet the "real thing" of the primordial psychic sphere. Even in this sphere the "real thing" becomes constituted at a higher level, as a causal thing, an identical substrate of causal properties (a "substance"). Obviously substance and causality indicate constitutional problems of a higher level. The constitutional problem of the thing pertaining to the senses, along with the problem of the spatiality and temporality that are fundamen-tally essential to it, is precisely the problem just now indi-cated. It is a problem of descriptive inquiry that concerns only the synthetic complexes of thing-appearances (apparencies, perspective aspects). Moreover, it is one-sided. The other side concerns the relation of the appearances back to the functioning animate organism, which in turn must be described in respect of its self-constitution and the signal peculiarity of its consti-tutive system of appearances.

When we proceed in this manner, new problems of descriptive explication continually arise, all of which must be solved system-atically if even the constitution of the primordial "world", as a world of "realities" — along with the great problem of the constitution of spatiality and temporality, as essential to "realities" in that world — is to be dealt with seriously. As its execution shows, this task alone comprises a tremendous province of investigations; still it furnishes only the underlying level for a full phenomenology of Nature, as Objective and yet as pure Nature — which itself is far from being the concrete world.

Our discussion of psychology has given us occasion to translate the distinction between what is primordial and what is constituted as alien into terms of the purely psychic and to sketch as psychological problems (though only hastily) the problems relating to a primordial, and to an Objective, Nature.

If, however, we return to the transcendental attitude, our outlines of the problems relating to the psychological origin of the "idea of space", and the like, provide us conversely with outlines for the parallel problems of transcendental phenomenology — namely the problems involved in a concrete explication of primordial Nature and the primordial world as a whole. This fills a great gap in our earlier statement of the problems relating <173> to / constitution of the world as a transcendental phenomenon.

The extraordinarily vast complex of researches pertaining to the primordial world makes up a whole discipline, which we may designate as "transcendental aesthetics" in a very much broadened sense. We adopt the Kantian title here because the space and time arguments of the critique of reason obviously, though in an extraordinarily restricted and unclarified manner, have in view a noematic Apriori of sensuous intuition. Broadened to comprise the concrete Apriori of (primordial) Nature, as given in purely sensuous intuition, it then requires phenomenological transcendental supplementation by incorporation into a complex of constitutional problems. On the other hand, it would not be consistent with the sense of the correlative Kantian title, "transcendental analytics", if we used this as a name for the upper stories of the constitutional Apriori, which pertain to the *Objective* world itself and the multiplicities constituting it (at the highest level, the Apriori pertaining to the "idealizing" and theorizing acts that ultimately constitute scientific Nature and the scientific world). The theory of experiencing someone else, the theory of so-called "empathy", belongs in the first story above our "transcendental aesthetics". There is need only to indicate that what we said about the psychological problems of origin in the lower story applies here as well: For the first time, the problem of empathy has been given its true sense, and the true method for its solution has been furnished, by constitutional phenomenology. Precisely on that account all previous theories (including Max Scheler's) have failed to give an actual solution, and it has never been recognized that the otherness of "someone else" becomes extended to the whole world, as its "Objectivity", giving it this sense in the first place.

We would also state expressly that it would of course be pointless to treat the positive science of *intentional psychology* and *transcendental phenomenology separately.* Obviously the work of actual execution must devolve upon the latter, whereas psychology, unconcerned about the Copernican shift, will take over the results. Yet it is important to note that, just as the psyche and the whole Objective world do not / lose their existence and ‹174› existential sense when considered transcendentally (since they are merely rendered originarily understandable, by the uncovering of their concrete all-sidedness), so positive psychology does not lose its rightful content but rather, freed of naïve positivity, becomes a discipline within universal transcendental philosophy itself. From this point of view we may say that, among the sciences that have been raised above the level of naïve positivity, intentional psychology is intrinsically the first.

Indeed, it enjoys yet another advantage over all other positive sciences. If it is built up in the positive attitude according to the right method of intentional analysis, it can have no "problems of fundamentals", like those that infect the other positive sciences: problems that arise from the one-sidedness of naïvely constituted Objectivity, which finally demands that, in order to attain all-sidedness, we shift to a transcendental consideration of the world. But intentional psychology already has the transcendental hiddenly within itself; only a final clarification of its sense is needed in order to make the Copernican shift, which does not change the content of psychology's intentional results but only leads back to its "ultimate sense". Psychology has just one fundamental problem [*Fundamental-problem*], which (it may be objected) is ultimately a problem of fundamentals [*Grundlagenproblem*], albeit the only one: the concept of the psyche..

§ 62. *Survey of our intentional explication of experiencing someone else.*

Let us return now, at the conclusion of this chapter, to the objection by which at first we let ourselves be guided, the objection to our phenomenology, so far as, from the very beginning, it claimed to be transcendental philosophy and, as such, to have the ability to solve the problems that concern the possibility of Objective knowledge. The objection runs as follows. Starting from the transcendental ego of the phenomenological reduction and thenceforth restricted to him, phenomenology is incapable of solving those problems. Without admitting that it does so, it lapses into a transcendental solipsism; and the whole step leading to other subjectivity and to genuine Objectivity is possible only by virtue of an unacknowledged metaphysics, a concealed adoption of Leibnizian traditions. /

‹175›   Our actual explications have dissipated the objection as groundless. The following is to be noted above all. At no point was the transcendental attitude, the attitude of transcendental epoché, abandoned; and our "theory" of experiencing someone else, our "theory" of experiencing others, did not aim at being and was not at liberty to be anything but explication of the sense, "others", as it arises from the constitutive productivity of that experiencing: the sense [1], "truly existing others", as it arises from the corresponding harmonious syntheses. What I demonstrate to myself harmoniously as "someone else" and therefore have given to me, by necessity and not by choice, as an actuality to be acknowledged, is *eo ipso* the existing Other for me in the transcendental attitude: the alter ego demonstrated precisely within the experiencing intentionality of my ego. Within the bounds of positivity we say and find it obvious that, in my own experience, I experience not only myself but others — in the particular form: experiencing someone else. The indubitable [2]

---

[1] Reading, with Typescript C, "*des Sinnes*", instead of "*des Limes*" (the limit). Cf. the French: "*le sens*".

[2] Reading with Typescript C, "*zweifellose*" instead of "*zweifellos*" (indubitably).

transcendental explication showed us not only that this positive statement is transcendentally legitimate but also that the concretely apprehended transcendental ego (who first becomes aware of himself, with his undetermined horizon, when he effects transcendental reduction) grasps himself in his own primordial being, and likewise (in the form of his transcendental experience of what is alien) grasps others: *other transcendental egos*, though they are given, not originaliter and in unqualifiedly apodictic evidence, but only in an evidence belonging to "external" experience. "In" myself I experience and know the Other; in me he becomes constituted — appresentatively mirrored, not constituted as the original. Hence it can very well be said, in a *broadened* sense, that the ego acquires — that I, as the one who meditatingly explicates, acquire by "self-explication" (explication of what I find in myself) every transcendency: as a transcendentally constituted transcendency and not as a transcendency accepted with naïve positivity. Thus the *illusion* vanishes: that *everything I*, qua transcendental ego, *know* [1] *as existing in consequence of myself* [2], and explicate as *constituted in myself*, must *belong to me as part of my own essence*. This is true only of "immanent transcendencies". As a title for the systems of synthetic actuality and potentiality that confer sense and being on me as ego in my own essentialness, constitution signifies constitution of immanent objective actuality. *At the start | of phenomenology*, when my attitude is that of <176> someone who is *only starting*, who is instituting phenomenological reduction for the first time, as a universal condition under which to pursue constitutional research, *the transcendental ego who comes into view is, to be sure, grasped apodictically* — but as having *a quite undetermined horizon*, a horizon restricted only by the general requirement that the world and all I know about it shall become a mere "phenomenon". Consequently, when I am starting in this manner, all those distinctions are lacking which are made only subsequently by intentional explication but which nevertheless (as I now see) pertain to me essentially. There is lacking, above all, self-understanding with respect to my primordial essence, my sphere of ownness in the pregnant

---

[1] Reading, with Typescript C, *"erkenne"* instead of *"erkennen"*.
[2] Reading, with Typescript C, *"aus mir selbst"* instead of simply *"mir selbst"*.

sense, and with respect to what, within that sphere itself, becomes constituted as an Other in experiencing someone else, as
something appresented but essentially non-given (and never to
become given) within my primordial sphere. I must first explicate *my own as such, in order to understand that, within my own,
what is not my own likewise receives existential sense* — and does
so as something appresented analogically. Therefore at the beginning I, the meditator, do not understand how I shall ever
attain others and myself ‹as one among others›, since all other
men are "parenthesized". At bottom moreover I do not yet
understand, and I recognize only reluctantly, that, when I
"parenthesize" myself qua man and qua human person, I
myself am nevertheless to be retained qua ego. Thus I can as
yet know nothing about a transcendental intersubjectivity;
involutarily I take myself, the ego, to be a *solus ipse* and still
regard all constitutional components as merely contents of this
one ego, even after I have acquired an initial understanding of
constitutive performances. The further explications made in the
present chapter were therefore necessary. Thanks to them, the
*full and proper sense of phenomenological transcendental "ideal-
ism" becomes understandable* to us for the first time. The *illusion*
of a solipsism is dissolved, *even though* the proposition that
everything existing for me must derive its existential sense
exclusively from me myself, from my sphere of consciousness
retains its validity and fundamental importance. Phenomenological transcendental idealism has presented itself as a *monad-
ology*, which, despite all our deliberate suggestions of Leibniz's
‹177› metaphysics, / draws its content purely from phenomenological
explication of the transcendental experience laid open by
transcendental reduction, accordingly from the most originary
evidence, wherein all conceivable evidences must be grounded —
or from the most originary legitimacy, which is the source of all
legitimacies and, in particular, all legitimacies of knowledge.
Actually, therefore, phenomenological explication is nothing
like "metaphysical construction"; and it is neither overtly nor
covertly a theorizing with adopted presuppositions or helpful
thoughts drawn from the historical metaphysical tradition. It
stands in sharpest contrast to all that, because it proceeds within
the limits of pure "intuition", or rather of pure sense-explication

based on a fulfilling givenness of the sense itself. Particularly in
the case of the Objective world of realities (as well as in the case
of each of the many ideal Objective worlds, which are the fields
of purely apriori sciences) — and this cannot be emphasized
often enough — phenomenological explication does nothing but
*explicate the sense this world has for us all, prior to any philoso-
phizing*, and obviously gets solely from our experience — *a sense
which philosophy can uncover but never alter*, and which, because
of an essential necessity, not because of our weakness, entails
(in the case of any actual experience) horizons that need fundamental clarification.

CONCLUSION

§ 63. *The task of criticizing transcendental experience and
knowledge.*

In the investigations of this meditation and already in those
of the two preceding meditations, we have been moving within
the realm of transcendental experience, of self-experience proper
and experience of someone else. We have trusted transcendental
experience because of its originarily lived-through evidence; and
similarly we have trusted the evidence of predicative description
and [1] all the other modes of evidence belonging to transcendental science. Meanwhile we have lost sight of the demand, so
seriously made at the beginning — namely that an *apodictic*
knowledge, as the only "genuinely scientific" knowledge,[2] be
achieved; but we have by no means dropped it. Only we preferred / to sketch in outline the tremendous wealth of problems ‹178›
belonging to the *first stage of phenomenology* — a stage which in
its own manner is itself *still infected with a certain naïveté (the
naïveté of apodicticity)* but contains the great and most characteristic accomplishment of phenomenology, as a refashioning
of science on a higher level — instead of entering into the
further and ultimate problems of phenomenology: those pertaining
to its *self-criticism*, which aims at determining not only the

---

[1] Supplied in accordance with Typescript C and the French translation.
[2] Reading, with Typescript C, *"eine apodiktische Erkenntnis, als die allein 'echt
wissenschaftliche' "*, instead of *"einer apodiktischen Erkenntnis, als der allein echt
wissenschaftlichen"*, which is syntactically impossible.

range and *limits* but also the *modes of apodicticity*. At least a preliminary idea of the kind of criticism of transcendental-phenomenological knowledge required here is given by our earlier indications of how, for example, a criticism of transcendental recollection discovers in it an apodictic content. All transcendental-philosophical theory of knowledge, as *"criticism of knowledge", leads back ultimately to criticism of transcendental-phenomenological knowledge* (in the first place, criticism of transcendental experience); and, owing to the essential reflexive relation of phenomenology to itself, this criticism also demands a criticism. In this connexion, however, there exist no endless regresses that are infected with difficulties of any kind (to say nothing of absurdities), despite the evident possibility of re-iterable transcendental reflections and criticisms.

§ 64. *Concluding word*.

Our meditations, we may venture to say, have in the main fulfilled their purpose, namely to show the concrete possibility of the Cartesian idea [1] of a philosophy as an all-embracing science grounded on an absolute foundation. To exhibit this concrete possibility, to show the feasibility ‹of such a philosophy› — though of course in the form of an endless program — means exhibiting a necessary and indubitable beginning and an equally necessary and always employable method — whereby, at the same time, a systematic order of all sensful problems is predelineated. This much we have actually done. The only things that remain are the easily understandable ramifications of transcendental phenomenology — as a beginning philosophy that grows and branches out into particular Objective sciences ‹179› — and its relation to the sciences of naïve positivity, which are given beforehand as examples. We now direct our attention to these sciences.

Daily practical living is naïve. It is immersion in the already-given world, whether it be experiencing, or thinking, or valuing, or acting. Meanwhile all those productive intentional functions

---

[1] Reading *"der Cartesianischen Idee"*, instead of *"die Cartesianische Idee"* (the concrete possibility, the Cartesian idea), as in both the published text and Typescript C. Cf. the French: *"de l'idée cartésienne"*.

of experiencing, because of which physical things are simply there, go on anonymously. The experiencer knows nothing about them, and likewise nothing about his productive thinking. The numbers, the predicative complexes of affairs, the goods, the ends, the works, present themselves because of the hidden performances; they are built up, member by member; they alone are regarded. Nor is it otherwise in the positive sciences. They are naïvetés of a higher level. They are the products of an ingenious theoretical technique; but the intentional performances from which everything ultimately originates remain unexplicated. To be sure, science claims the ability to justify its theoretical steps and is based throughout on criticism. But its criticism is not ultimate criticism of knowledge. The latter criticism is a study and criticism of the original productions, an uncovering of all their intentional horizons; and thus alone can the "range" of evidences be ultimately grasped and, correlatively, the existence-sense of objects, of theoretical formations, of goods and ends, be evaluated. Consequently we have — and precisely at the high level attained by modern positive sciences — problems of fundamentals, paradoxes, unintelligibilities. The primitive concepts, which pervade the whole science and determine the sense of its sphere of objects and the sense of its theories, originated naïvely; they have undetermined intentional horizons; they are products of unknown, only crudely and naïvely exercised intentional functions. That is true, not only in the case of the *special sciences*, but also in the case of *traditional logic*, with all its formal norms. Every attempt of the historically developed sciences to attain a better grounding or a better understanding of their own sense and performance is a bit of self-investigation on the part of the scientist. But there is only one *radical* self-investigation, and it is phenomenological. Radical self-investigation and completely universal self-investigation are inseparable from one another and at the same time inseparable from the genuine phenomenological method of self-investigation, in the form peculiar to transcendental reduction: intentional self-explication of the transcendental ego, who is made accessible by transcendental reduction, and / systematic ‹180› description in the logical form of an intuitive eidetics. But universal and eidetic self-explication signifies mastery of all the conceivable constitutive possibilities "innate" in the ego and in a transcendental intersubjectivity.

Therefore a consequentially progressing phenomenology constructs a priori (yet with a strictly *intuited* essential necessity and universality), on the one hand, the *forms* of conceivable worlds and, on the other hand, conceivable worlds themselves, within the limits set by all conceivable forms of being and by their system of levels. But it constructs them "originarily" — that is: in correlation with the constitutional Apriori, the Apriori of the intentional performances that constitute them.

Since, with its procedure, phenomenology has no already-given actualities or concepts of actualities, but from the very beginning derives its concepts from the originariness of the constitutive performance (which is itself conceived in originary concepts), and since, owing to the necessity that all horizons be uncovered, it is also cognizant of all differences in range, all abstract relativities: therefore it must attain by itself the concept-systems that determine the fundamental sense of all scientific provinces. The concepts making up those systems predelineate all the formal demarcations that pertain to the form-idea of any possible world of being whatever. Hence they must be the *genuine* concepts that are *fundamental* to all sciences. In the case of concepts fashioned originarily in this manner, there can be no paradoxes. This is true of all the fundamental concepts that concern the concrete structure and the total structural form of sciences that relate (or can become related) to the various regions of being. Thus the investigations concerning the transcendental constitution of a world, which we have roughly indicated in these meditations, are precisely *the beginning of a radical clarification of the sense and origin* (or of the sense in consequence of the origin) *of the concepts: world, Nature, space, time, psychophysical being, man, psyche, animate organism, social community, culture*, and so forth. It is plain that the actual carrying out of the indicated investigations would have to lead to all the concepts which, as unexplored, function as fundamental concepts in all positive sciences, but which accrue ‹181› in phenomenology with an all-round clarity and / distinctness that leave no further room for any conceivable questionableness.

We can now say likewise that, in apriori transcendental phenomenology, all apriori sciences without exception originate with an ultimate grounding, thanks to its correlational research, and that, taken with this origin, they belong *within an all-embracing apriori phenomenology itself*, as its systematically differentiated *branches*. This system of the all-embracing Apriori is therefore to be designated also as the systematic *unfolding of the all-embracing Apriori* innate in the essence of a transcendental subjectivity (and consequently in that of a transcendental intersubjectivity) — or as the systematic unfolding of the *universal logos of all conceivable being*. In other words: As developed systematically and fully, transcendental phenomenology would be *ipso facto* the true and *genuine universal ontology* — not, however, just an emptily formal universal ontology, but also one that comprised in itself all regional existential possibilities, and did so in respect of all the *correlations* pertaining to them.

This universal *concrete* ontology (or universal and concrete *theory of science* — this concrete logic of being) would therefore be the intrinsically first *universe of science* grounded on an absolute foundation. In respect of order, the intrinsically first of the philosophical disciplines would be "solipsistically" reduced "egology", the egology of the primordially reduced ego. Then only would come intersubjective phenomenology, which is founded on that discipline; moreover it would start with a generality that at first treated the universal questions, and only subsequently would it branch out into the apriori sciences.

This total science of the Apriori would then be *the foundation for genuine sciences of matters of fact* and for a *genuine all-embracing philosophy* in the Cartesian sense: an all-embracing science of the factually existent, grounded on an absolute foundation. All the rationality of the fact lies, after all, in the Apriori. Apriori science is the science of radical universalities and necessities, to which the science of matter of fact must have recourse, precisely in order that it may ultimately become grounded on such radical principles. But apriori science must not be naïve; on the contrary, it / must have originated from ‹182› ultimate transcendental-phenomenological sources and be

fashioned accordingly into an all-round Apriori, resting on itself
and justifying itself by itself.

Finally, lest any misunderstanding arise, I would point out
that, as already stated, phenomenology indeed *excludes every
naïve metaphysics* that operates with absurd things in themselves,
but *does not exclude metaphysics as such*. It does no violence to
the problem-motives that inwardly drive the old tradition into
the wrong line of inquiry and the wrong method; and it by no
means professes to stop short of the "supreme and ultimate"
questions. The intrinsically first being, the being that precedes
and bears every worldly Objectivity, is transcendental intersubjectivity: the universe of monads, which effects its communion in various forms. But, within the de facto monadic
sphere and (as an ideal possibility) within every conceivable
monadic sphere, occur *all the problems of accidental factualness,
of death, of fate*, of the possibility of a *"genuine" human life*
demanded as "meaningful" in a particular sense — among them,
therefore, the problem of the "meaning" of history —, and all
the further and still higher problems. We can say that they are
the *ethico-religious* problems, but stated in the realm where
everything that can have a possible sense for us must be
stated.

Thus the idea of an all-embracing philosophy becomes actualized — quite differently than Descartes and his age, guided
by modern natural science, expected: Not as an all-embracing
system of deductive theory, as though everything that exists
were included in the unity of a computation, but — with a
radical alteration of the fundamentally essential sense of all
science — as a system of *phenomenological* disciplines, which
treat correlative themes and are ultimately grounded, not on an
axiom, ego cogito, but on an *all-embracing self-investigation*.

In other words: The path leading to a knowledge absolutely
grounded in the highest sense, or (this being the same thing) a
philosophical knowledge, is necessarily the path of universal
self-knowledge — first of all monadic, and then intermonadic.
We can say also that a radical and universal continuation of
‹183› Cartesian meditations, or (equivalently) a / universal self-
cognition, is philosophy itself and encompasses all self-accounta-
ble science.

The Delphic motto, "Know thyself!" has gained a new signification. Positive science is a science lost in the world. I must lose the world by epoché, in order to regain it by a universal self-examination. *"Noli foras ire,"* says Augustine, *"in te redi, in interiore homine habitat veritas."* [1]

---

[1] Do not wish to go out; go back into yourself. Truth dwells in the inner man. — *De vera religione*, 39, n. 72.

Husserliana

EDMUND HUSSERL – GESAMMELTE WERKE

1. **Cartesianische Meditationen und Pariser Vorträge.** Hrsg. und eingeleitet von Stephan Strasser. Nachdruck der 2. verb. Auflage, 1973
   ISBN 90-247-0214-3
2. **Die Idee der Phänomenologie.** Fünf Vorlesungen. Hrsg. und eingeleitet von Walter Biemel. Nachdruck der 2. erg. Auflage, 1973
   ISBN 90-247-5139-X
3. **Ideen zu einer reinen Phänomenologie und phänomenologischen Philosophie.** *Erstes Buch:* Allgemeine Einführung in die reine Phänomenologie. 1. Halbband: Text der 1.-3. Auflage; 2. Halbband: Ergänzende Texte (1912-1929). Neu hrsg. von Karl Schuhmann. Nachdruck, 1976
   Set ISBN 90-247-1912-7
4. **Ideen zu einer reinen Phänomenologie und phänomenologischen Philosophie.** *Zweites Buch:* Phänomenologische Untersuchungen zur Konstitution. Hrsg. von Marly Biemel. Nachdruck, 1984   ISBN 90-247-0218-6
5. **Ideen zu einer reinen Phänomenologie und phänomenologischen Philosophie.** *Drittes Buch:* Die Phänomenologie und die Fundamente der Wissenschaften. Hrsg. von Marly Biemel. Nachdruck, 1971
   ISBN 90-247-0219-4
6. **Die Krisis der europäischen Wissenschaften und die transzendentale Phänomenologie.** Eine Einleitung in die phänomenologische Philosophie. Hrsg. von Walter Biemel. Nachdruck der 2. verb. Auflage, 1976
   ISBN 90-247-0221-6
7. **Erste Philosophie (1923/24).** *Erster Teil:* Kritische Ideengeschichte. Hrsg. von Rudolf Boehm 1956   ISBN 90-247-0223-2
8. **Erste Philosophie (1923/24).** *Zweiter Teil:* Theorie der phänomenologischen Reduktion. Hrsg. von Rudolf Boehm. 1959   ISBN 90-247-0225-9
9. **Phänomenologische Psychologie.** Vorlesungen Sommersemester 1925. Hrsg. von Walter Biemel. 2. verb. Auflage, 1968   ISBN 90-247-0226-7
10. **Zur Phänomenologie des inneren Zeitbewußtseins (1893-1917).** Hrsg. von Rudolf Boehm. Nachdruck der 2. verb. Auflage, 1969
    ISBN 90-247-0227-5
11. **Analysen zur passiven Synthesis.** Aus Vorlesungs- und Forschungsmanuskripten (1918-1926). Hrsg. von Margot Fleischer. 1966
    ISBN 90-247-0229-1
12. **Philosophie der Arithmetik.** Mit ergänzenden Texten (1890-1901). Hrsg. von Lothar Eley. 1970   ISBN 90-247-0230-5
13. **Zur Phänomenologie der Intersubjektivität.** Texte aus dem Nachlaß. *Erster Teil:* 1905-1920. Hrsg. von Iso Kern. 1973   ISBN 90-247-0230-5
14. **Zur Phänomenologie der Intersubjektivität.** Texte aus dem Nachlaß. *Zweiter Teil:* 1921-1928. Hrsg. von Iso Kern. 1973   ISBN 90-247-5029-6
15. **Zur Phänomenologie der Intersubjektivität.** Texte aus dem Nachlaß. *Dritter Teil:* 1929-1935. Hrsg. von Iso Kern. 1973   ISBN 90-247-5030-X

Husserliana

EDMUND HUSSERL – GESAMMELTE WERKE

Kluwer Academic Publishers – Dordrecht / Boston / London

CPSIA information can be obtained at www.ICGtesting.com
Printed in the USA
240072LV00001B/98/A